Dick Francis

Twayne's English Authors Series

Kinley E. Roby, Editor
Northeastern University

TEAS 464

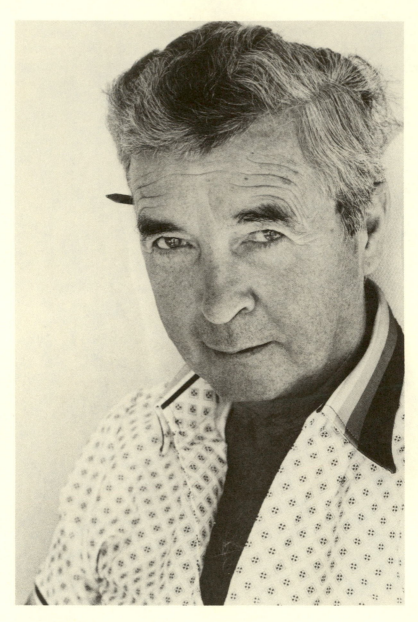

DICK FRANCIS
© 1988 David Vance/*Interview*.
Used by permission.

Dick Francis

By J. Madison Davis

Pennsylvania State University,
The Behrend College

Twayne Publishers
A Division of G. K. Hall & Co. • *Boston*

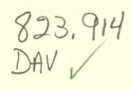

Dick Francis

J. Madison Davis

Copyright 1989 by G. K. Hall & Co.
All rights reserved.
Published by Twayne Publishers
A Division of G. K. Hall & Co.
70 Lincoln Street
Boston, Massachusetts 02111

Copyediting supervised by Barbara Sutton
Book production by Gabrielle B. McDonald
Book design by Barbara Anderson

Typeset in 11 pt. Garamond
by Williams Press, Inc., Albany, New York

Printed on permanent/durable acid-free paper
and bound in the United States of America

Library of Congress Cataloging–in–Publication Data

Davis, J. Madison.
    Dick Francis / by J. Madison Davis.
        p.   cm.—(Twayne's English authors series ; TEAS 464)
    Bibliography: p.
    Includes index.
    ISBN 0-8057-6970-6
    1. Francis, Dick—Criticism and interpretation.   2. Detective and
mystery stories, English—History and criticism.   3. Horse-racing in
literature.   I. Title.   II. Series.
PR6056.R27Z666   1989
823'.914—dc19   88–24825
                                                                      CIP

For Jimmie and Joncy,
like most of my other work

Contents

About the Author

J. Madison Davis is a fiction writer, as well as a critic, who has always been fond of the mystery. He has studied writing and literature at Franklin and Marshall College, the University of Maryland, Johns Hopkins University, and the University of Southern Mississippi. He has published much nonfiction on a broad variety of subjects, in periodicals such as *Shakespeare Quarterly, Early American Life, Mississippi Folklore Register, Extrapolation*, and *Studies in American Drama, 1945–Present*. His short stories have appeared in *Seattle Review, Pulpsmith, Mississippi Review, Antietam Review, Antithesis*, in the anthologies *From Mt. San Angelo* and *New Southern Writing*, and in many other publications. His reviews of current fiction have appeared in *Denver Quarterly, Bloomsbury Review, New Orleans Review, Texas Review*, and others.

Davis is also the author of *Stanislaw Lem: A Reader's Guide* (Starmont House) and is coeditor (with Philip C. Kolin) of *Critical Essays on Edward Albee* (G. K. Hall). His own mystery-thriller, *The Murder of Frau Schütz*, was published in October 1988 by Walker and Company. He is at work on *Conversations with Robertson Davies* (University Press of Mississippi) and another novel. He is an associate professor of English at Pennsylvania State University in Erie, Behrend College, where he teaches modern art, fiction writing, and modern world literature. He has been the recipient of residencies at the Virginia Center for the Creative Arts, the Hambidge Center for the Creative Arts and Sciences, and the Ragdale Foundation. He has also received a grant for his fiction writing from the Pennsylvania Council of the Arts in 1984 and one from the Canadian Embassy's Faculty Research Program in 1987 for his work on Robertson Davies.

Preface

This is the first book-length study of Dick Francis's writing, and it was written with the intention of creating a better appreciation for the underlying structures and moral paradigms that are part of his fiction. There is so much simple entertainment in a Francis novel that it is easy to overlook a number of these elements, but the tough, clean, plain style is deceptive and closely follows Hemingway's dictum that prose should be like an iceberg, the greater part of it submerged. Drawing on the Francis novels' obvious affinity with the tradition of the hard-boiled detective novel, I have examined all of the novels and short stories, comparing them to each other and to the larger tradition. The novels that best illustrate particular points are studied in great detail as to their relation to the issues under scrutiny. Other novels are brought into the discussion as necessary. In this way, all of his fiction has been included. I have also paid particular attention to the relationships between Francis's own fascinating life and his fiction. He draws predominantly and insistently on personal experience in creating his fictions and frequently unashamedly reveals the factual connections in his autobiography and in interviews. His personal history has also had a profound effect on the shaping of his moral vision, and I have tried to elucidate some of these connections. Reading his novels becomes a long conversation with the man behind them, and, at least as he is revealed by them, we come to appreciate the man himself much more than we would most other novelists. Readers do not just get to like Francis novels; they get to like Dick Francis.

A novel a year is an arduous schedule, and, as might be expected, it soon becomes apparent that Francis relies on an amiable formula for creating his fiction. It became the purpose of my study to examine the nature of his formula, to probe some of its philosophical implications, to see why his novels are perennial favorites. The word *formula* seems to conjure up the tedious notion of hack authors endlessly—and artlessly—repeating themselves. Yet the notion that an author must explore radically new forms is a prejudicial hangover from romanticism and the concept of the artist as avant-garde. Francis was mercifully free of aesthetic pretense when he chose to start his first novel. An utter amateur, he had written little but letters since he left school at age fifteen, but he had always enjoyed thrillers and thought he would like to write one. Immediately he adopted a structure that suited his personality and what he wished to say, and it spoke to a large public. His natural restlessness and intelligence, as well as his integrity, however, make him travel far up certain avenues within the formula in order to avoid repetition and to avoid disappointing his legions of loyal fans.

Each novel is a thoroughbred; it inherits certain traits, yet each runs a little differently. Each has a slightly different coloring or shape or temperament, yet it comes from the same sire, who always breeds well. Another way of looking at it is to make an analogy with art of the preromantic periods, when musicians, for example, worked within carefully structured forms. The greatest of them—Bach, Handel, Haydn, and some others—are always surprising with what they accomplish within their strict conceptions, while many of their comrades were woefully predictable. I often think of Francis as a master of themes and variations. Somewhere in the background of all the differences, the original theme can be heard, and the reader's delight is in both its divergence and its congruence.

One of the most tiresome aspects of academic criticism is that professors are always pretending that their subjects deserve a niche in the pantheon of great literature. I will not pretend that the Dick Francis mysteries are superior to the works of novelists like Gabriel García-Márquez and Doris Lessing or that they have the philosophical weight of André Malraux and Thomas Mann—not even Francis himself would say such a thing, even if several glasses of champagne and winning a long-shot trifecta made him heady. Yet the practice of classifying novels into categories like literary, mystery, horror, and romance does result in his accomplishments' being undervalued simply because of the genre, and the very fact of his extraordinary popularity immediately causes mandarins who make such judgments recoil. I confess I feel the same reticence about best-sellers (so many are atrocities of language and taste), indeed about anything that is wildly popular, and yet Francis won me over easily, long before I set about to write this book. His best novels— *Reflex, Nerve,* and *Odds Against*—are as complex as and certainly more profound than many of the whining, award-winning introspections that readers endure like a dose of cod liver oil. Francis, already extremely popular, deserves to be more popular. Even his worst novels are at a level that should push many other books off the shelf and into the dustbin. Even his worst novels are concise, convey strong feeling, and are composed with obvious sentence-by-sentence craftsmanship. He never takes his audience for granted or underestimates the difficulty of effective writing; his care is apparent in almost every word. His prose uses deceptive simplicity for powerful effect. To my mind, he is one of the best living popular writers.

When I was approached about doing this book, I had already many times delighted in the novels of Dick Francis. A friend, thriller novelist and horse lover Carolyn Banks (*Mr. Right, The Darkroom,* and *The Girls on the Row*), had recommended Francis to me, and I was reminded of her praise when I saw a copy of *Risk* stuck haphazardly on a shelf at K-Mart. At 1 A.M. that night, I staggered red-eyed to bed, knowing that I would not only mumble my way through the next day's teaching but that I would likely be up again the next night in order to find out the solution to Roland Britten's mysterious kidnapping. Since then, I have frequently found myself in a similar situation, sitting down after the news, planning to read two, maybe three chapters, then discovering with a shock I have gone halfway through another novel and another night.

That will not happen again, at least for a while, but I am not happy to say so. To do this study, I have read all of the two dozen Dick Francis mysteries at least twice, and I intend to rest up until the next one comes along, fully expecting that it will deliver another evening as delightful as all the others. Frankly I expected by the time I had gotten through all those pages to have become bored with him, but I am not the first fool who has underestimated him. Francis has never failed to win, place, or at least show in a crowded field of mystery competitors. Not only are these novels bought and read, but even in our disposable society they are kept or continuously recirculated. The public libraries have waiting lists, and sellers of new books always have a good two feet of Francis on the shelf. A local used-book dealer told me, "Francis? Oh, we get him, but he goes fast." I hope the following commentaries will help readers to appreciate him even more.

J. Madison Davis

Pennsylvania State University,
The Behrend College

Acknowledgments

I would like to express my appreciation to John Coleman for his research assistance, to Carol Griffiths and Archie K. Loss for their advice, to Provost John M. Lilley of Pennsylvania State University in Erie for the research support, and to the various members of the Mississippi Philological Association and the Popular Culture Association for their comments on the excerpts I read at their annual meetings.

I would also like to thank Houghton Mifflin Co. and Hamish Hamilton, Ltd., for permission to quote from "The Simple Art of Murder" in *The Simple Art of Murder* by Raymond Chandler. Copyright 1950 by Raymond Chandler. Copyright © renewed 1978 by Helga Greene. Reprinted by permission of Houghton Mifflin Co. and Hamish Hamilton, Ltd.

I would also like to thank Harper & Row, Publishers, Inc., and Michael Joseph, Ltd., for permission to quote from the following books by Dick Francis: *Blood Sport,* copyright © 1967 by Dick Francis; *Bonecrack,* copyright © 1971 by Dick Francis; *Dead Cert,* copyright © 1962 by Dick Francis; *Enquiry,* copyright © 1969 by Dick Francis; *Flying Finish,* copyright © 1966 by Dick Francis; *For Kicks,* copyright © 1965 by Dick Francis; *Forfeit,* copyright © 1969 by Dick Francis; *In the Frame,* copyright © 1976 by Dick Francis; *Knockdown,* copyright © 1974 by Dick Francis; *Nerve,* copyright © 1964 by Dick Francis; *Odds Against,* copyright © 1965 by Dick Francis; *Rat Race,* copyright © 1971 by Dick Francis; *Risk,* copyright © 1977 by Dick Francis; *Slayride,* copyright © 1973 by Dick Francis; *Smokescreen,* copyright © 1972 by Dick Francis; *The Sport of Queens,* copyright © 1957, revised version copyright © 1981 by Dick Francis; and *Whip Hand,* copyright © 1979 by Dick Francis. Reprinted by permission of Harper & Row, Publishers, Inc., and Michael Joseph, Ltd.

I would also like to thank the Putnam Publishing Group and Michael Joseph, Ltd., for permission to quote from the following novels by Dick Francis: *Banker,* copyright © 1983 by Dick Francis; *Break In,* copyright © 1986 by Dick Francis; *The Danger,* copyright © 1983 by Dick Francis; and *Reflex,* copyright © 1981 by Dick Francis. Reprinted by permission of the Putnam Publishing Group and Michael Joseph, Ltd.

Chronology

1920 Richard Stanley Francis born 31 October at his grandfather's farm in Wales.

1933 First serious riding accident breaks teeth, palate, jaw, and nose. Afterward rides ponies for circus owner.

1935 Drops out of Maidenhead County School. Wins at hunter class show substituting for father.

1938 Family purchases its own stables.

1940 Volunteers for the Royal Air Force, serving as an airframe fitter and a pilot.

1946 Debuts as amateur jockey on Russian Hero.

1947 As an amateur jockey, wins first race after thirty-nine tries. Breaks collarbone. Marries Mary Margaret Brenchly.

1948 Becomes Professional National Hunt Jockey and second jockey for Lord Bicester.

1949 Mary Francis is stricken with polio. Rides Roimond to a second in Grand National.

1950 When jockey Lord Mildmay mysteriously disappears, Francis substitutes for him and begins relationship with trainer Peter Cazalet. This leads to his riding for the royal family.

1951 Eleven horses fall at first fence in Grand National, Francis's mount, Finnure, among them.

1954 Becomes National Hunt's Champion Jockey by winning 76 of 331 races. Sails to United States to ride in International Steeplechase at Belmont Park, New York.

1956 Clearly leading the Grand National, Francis's mount, Devon Loch, inexplicably comes to an abrupt halt. Francis is approached by literary agent for his autobiography.

1957 Retires from racing in February and publishes *The Sport of Queens*. Becomes racing correspondent for the *London Sunday Express*.

1962 *Dead Cert,* his first novel.

1964 *Nerve.*

1965   *For Kicks* receives Crime Writers' Association Silver Dagger Award. Also publishes *Odds Against*. Falls from horse, breaks collarbone for twelfth time, and cracks skull while judging Royal Show.

1968   *Forfeit*.

1969   *Forfeit* receives Edgar Allan Poe Award.

1973   Becomes chairman of the Crime Writers' Association. Retires from *Sunday Express*.

1974   *Dead Cert* made into film directed by Tony Richardson.

1978   "The Racing Game" filmed by Yorkshire Television.

1979   Success of television's "The Racing Game" inspires second Sid Halley novel. *Whip Hand* wins both Poe Award and Gold Dagger.

1980   Changes American publisher. Putnam's begins to market his novels as "mainstream" instead of "mysteries." *Reflex* spends three months on *New York Times* best-seller list.

1983   Knighted, Order of the British Empire.

1986   Biography of champion jockey Lester Piggott published.

1987   *Bolt*, his twenty-fifth novel, another best-seller.

1988   *Hot Money* rises to the top five on most best-seller lists.

Chapter One
The Rider Becomes Writer

The Formative Years

Imagine this for a scenario: a young Welsh boy wants more than anything else to be a jockey. He grows up a little too large for flat racing, however, and switches to steeplechasing. After a stint in the Royal Air Force during World War II, not only does he become a good rider, he becomes one of the best. The Queen Mother makes him her number one jockey. The culmination of his career comes about when he is assigned to ride the favorite in the Grand National, the world's most celebrated steeplechase. The horse, however, inexplicably bungles the race in the home stretch, and the jockey is bitterly disappointed. Age is catching up with him; he does not heal so readily after falls. He faces the awkward transition from champion to ordinary life. With the emotional support of his wife, he takes a job writing racing news and discovers he has a knack for words. When a publisher offers him a contract for his autobiography, the ex-jockey, despite his lack of education, insists upon writing it himself. His wife helps with the grammar. The book is a big success, but is it mostly because he was a star athlete? He writes a novel. It too sells extremely well, and our ex-jockey uses all of his knowledge of riding to become a best-selling author for two decades. Implausible? Certainly, but even more implausibly true.

Dick Francis was born on the last day of October in 1920 at Coedcanlas, his mother's father's farm, near Tenby, Wales,[1] in a region known as the "little England beyond Wales" because immigrants settled it in the Middle Ages and never bothered much with the Welsh language.[2] His memories of childhood days spent there are idyllic. The terrain rolled and provided land enough for childhood explorations and imaginary adventures beyond the carrying distance of adult voices. The house was old, with whitewashed walls six feet thick, and integrated itself into the countryside, unlike newer buildings. It had no electricity and no nearby shops, so there was always a bustle of activity. The

1

family made its own butter and cheese, baked bread, smoked hams, preserved fruits and vegetables, and brewed its own beer. Francis's grandparents were helped in this work by five children who frequently lived at the farm with their spouses (*SQ,* 14–15).

Francis and his brother Douglas learned to ride at a young age. They took donkeys on expeditions across Coedcanlas, and because his father had a theory that the best way to learn balance is to ride bareback and because there was no saddle for the donkey, young Dick learned to perch on its "high, bony back" at age five. His first "riding fee" consisted of a challenge from nine-year-old Douglas to leap a small rail fence while riding the donkey backward. The boy, saving to buy a toy farm, could not pass up the proffered sixpence. Dick tumbled to the ground several times in a foreshadowing of his future career, doubling up his brother in laughter. But Dick was, and would always be, tough. He persisted until he won the sixpence. He would later write, "In my heart, from that moment, I became a professional horseman" (*SQ,* 14).

His grandfather, Willie Thomas, rode to hounds two or three times a week, though Dick did not see the hunt often because his father could stay at the farm for only a few days at Christmas. When their visit coincided with a meet, Dick would pester someone to take him though he was too young to ride. Willie Thomas was kind, Francis tells us, and greatly loved by the people thereabouts, who felt free to drop by his house. He was also, however, "a great man in the Victorian tradition," who ruled over his children, "even after they had grown up and married" (*SQ,* 15), and whose idea of children was that they should be "seen but not heard." These observations are of some interest in considering the adult Francis's treatment of father and son relations in his novels.

Avid readers of Francis's novels cannot help but notice the often-strained relationships between fathers and sons (or the lack of a father altogether) and look for signs foreshadowing this in his autobiographical discussion of his father, George Vincent Francis. Dick's father and mother were both from Pembrokeshire in Southwest Wales. After returning from the Great War, however, George moved in order to find a job using his skills with hunting and show horses. After a few years at Bishop's, a fashionable stable, George became the successful manager of W. J. Smith's Hunting Stables at Holyport near Maidenhead outside London. Dick was seven at the time and lived there for the next ten years. He learned much about riding because of the different types of horses there, and even members of the royal family came down from London for riding lessons, which Dick and his brother watched closely. He met the queen when he was twelve and once was presented a riding crop as a prize by the Princess Elizabeth. The brothers never had a lesson themselves, but Dick recalls his father thundering directions such as, "Dick, keep your elbows *in*," and "Sit up boy, sit up" (*SQ,* 20), nearly the same words Edward Link of the novel *Smokescreen* will remember his father yelling.[3] Even when Dick won, George always said something indicating that the boy could have done better, something Francis writes was "designed to lower any high opinion I might be forming of myself" (*SQ,* 23). George seems to have balanced his roaring with giving his boys responsibility, however, and asking their opinions about particular horses. He gave Dick his first serious victory on a horse when, stricken by sciatica, he insisted the boy take his place. Showing any horse takes considerable subtle skill. This horse, Ballymonis, was a petulant creature with an unpredictable will. The owner and others were skeptical as they looked over the fourteen-year-old boy, but there was no time to find an adequate replacement. Dick won. In a paragraph that foreshadows many of the themes of his novels, Francis considers his father's manner of teaching:

I suppose the only thing which saved us from being horribly swollen-headed little boys was the knowledge drummed into us by Father, the nagsmen, and the ponies themselves, that however much we learned, there would always be more to learn. We were never allowed to be satisfied with what we achieved, never encouraged to think we were any good, always exhorted to greater efforts. I now know that these admonitions, instilled into me at such an early age, were very sensible. Year by year I still find that it is dangerous to begin to be complacent about one's skill; an unexpected and painful fall is a rough disillusionment. (*SQ,* 20–21)

If there is some implied coolness in the father, Francis clearly feels it is compensated for by the lesson about life. In the future, Dick would need this lesson many times. He developed a strong professional attitude toward riding. Since they did not own the horses they trained, Dick and his brother were always losing their equine friends and learned an acceptance of the losses life bestows on everyone. Another such lesson came when Dick's grandfather died (Dick was ten), and Coedcanlas was sold.

Dick's father was indifferent to his son's schooling. Only through his mother's persistence did the boy receive any education. The only time he preferred school was during the threshing season, when he was required to clean the dust from under the thresher. Even then he often managed to skip a couple of days a week, going fox hunting or to shows at every opportunity. At fourteen he determined to leave school altogether, but his mother insisted he stick it out for another year. He was particularly fond of hunting and remembers the freedom of the chase, polishing saddle and boots for Boxing Day, even his first "blooding" with sentimental affection (*SQ,* 24–25).

If the donkey at Coedcanlas received the honor of being the first of many quadrupeds to dump Dick unceremoniously, a horse named Tulip was the first to inflict serious injury on him. Dick's mother, Catherine Mary Francis (née Thomas), was more than ordinarily solicitous about Dick's health because he had developed pneumonia as a baby and frequently caught cold afterward. Her concern was also increased by his brother Douglas's having tubercular lesions on his lung, which allowed him to spend much of his life in the country air or by the sea. Dick frequently exploited the situation by playing ill, but Tulip put him in the hospital. Shortly after he got braces to correct the problem of a pair of oversized incisors, Dick was trying to calm the unruly show pony. It reared up and fell back on him. The saddle pommel smashed in braces and incisors and broke his jaw, palate, and nose.

Dick saw his injuries mostly as an opportunity to miss more school. As he began for the first of many times the process of knitting up bones, he was offered the chance of caring for and riding show ponies for a circus. He even practiced trying to balance standing on the rump of a moving pony and fantasized being an acrobat (*SQ,* 29). What his mother thought of all this, Francis does not tell us, but since her husband had been a jockey before World War I, her father-in-law a jockey, and her own father an avid huntsman, perhaps she was more comfortable to have Dick on a horse than near a runny nose. He does say that she disapproved of Dick's ambitions when he left school and asked his father to get him a job in a steeplechasing stable (*SQ,* 34), and after World War II, when he persisted in his wish, she told him she would always worry about his safety as a jockey and that he had no idea "how ruthless the racing world is" (*SQ,* 52). She and her husband also did not particularly relish Dick's being in apprenticeship, and they wished that he would grow taller than the usual flat-racing jockey (*SQ,* 32–33).

They got their wish: he grew eighteen inches in less than four years and became much too heavy and tall for flat racing. Not greatly disturbed, he determined to become a steeplechaser, for long legs are an advantage in keeping on a mount as it leaps hedges. His attempts to get associated with a jump stable, however, were frustrated. First, he was only sixteen. Then one man who had promised employment died in a car crash. There were no other openings. He could do nothing but wait, and waiting placed another delay in his path. In 1938 his father risked all their family capital to open his own stables, and Dick stuck with them, working harder than he ever had to help the family make a success of it. For a brief time, he rode a family friend's horses in point-to-points, but the man died. "Deeply disappointed, I was again an onlooker at the races," Francis writes, "with such envy and longing to be taking part myself, that they held no pleasure for me" (*SQ,* 38). He did not desert his family, however, something that may even be remarkable in a boy of eighteen whose sole passionate desire is to race. His loyalty and this fateful parade of obstacles to his racing eventually manifest themselves in the novels as his heroes frequently put aside their personal desires for the sake of family and as they almost too philosophically accept whatever obstacles block their fantasies.

"922385 A.C. Francis, R."

No obstacle, however, can be more fateful than war. When it begins, people are uncertain why. The young or the foolish usually cheer its onset in the belief that everything bad will be swept away; the old or the wiser know only that nothing will ever be the same. As the cataclysm of World War II increased, business at the Francis stables declined. There was little for Dick to do at home, so he decided to join the cavalry. But the cavalry did not want him. He wrote for help to friends in the Scots Greys in Edinburgh. Armed with their letters, he returned to the recruiting office, where an indifferent officer invited him to become an assistant cook. On an impulse, he returned and offered to fly. A different officer said he could become an air gunner or ground staff; they were not taking any pilots. "Pilot," said Dick, and the officer told him to sign on as an airframe fitter and then ask for a remuster. Francis later commented, "It was my first experience of the easy callous lying of the forces, and I did not recognise it. I believed him, and I signed. . . . . When I tried to re-muster I was laughed at for being so simple" (*SQ,* 39).

Like the heroes he would later create, however, Francis was as tenacious as a tick. While learning to repair and clean every part of an airplane except the engine, he applied every month to become a pilot. After a year he was called in for an interview, which turned into more of a lecture, and he was sent back to airframe fitting. Chasing back and forth in the North African campaign, he worked in the rubble of bombed airfields and spent much time hiding in trenches with his comrades while the enemy bombed their huts. Francis later wrote, "I acquired the sleeve propeller of an L.A.C. [leading aircraftman] and a lifelong distaste for sand. And every month I sent in an application to fly" (*SQ*, 40). Every six months, they interviewed him, and he tried to impress them with flying-type hobbies: birdwatching, kites, star gazing. When he finally told them the truth—"Huntin', shootin', and fishin' "—the squadron leader thought he was joking and ejected him from the room. Despising his job, he nonetheless became acquainted with an area of the world very different from Britain, spending much time in Cairo and occasionally hitchhiking to Tel Aviv, Beirut, Jerusalem, and Damascus. He even tried riding a camel, discovering seasickness in the swaying of the ship of the desert.

These little tales of absurdity are common to anyone who has experienced military life, and, of course, members of the armed forces in wartime are given a heightened recognition of absurdity in the philosophical sense as they daily hear of random death and meaningless gestures. This feeling for the inexplicable workings of fate is also an ingredient that Francis stirs into all of his stories. Ultimately, after El Alamein, headquarters gave in to his thirty-seven applications to be transferred, and he was shipped to Rhodesia for pilot training. Although his poor schooling made the math of navigation a terrible burden, alone in the air he felt the freedom he had always felt on horseback. The Tiger Moth fighter plane was like a horse with a tender mouth, he was told, and needed a light hand. He flew fighter escort for a while, but soon the Germans had little to harry the bombers with, so Francis was, unhappily, transferred to a Wellington bomber, which was more like "some weary old three-mile steeplechasers" (*SQ*, 43). He was also trained to fly troops across the Rhine in a glider, but only twenty courses of pilots were needed, and Francis was in the twenty-second. As the war ran down, Francis flew a kind of escort duty, helping surrendering ships into port, a boring job that almost resulted in his accidentally colliding with another plane. He also was trained to fly four-engine Lancasters before he returned home. "I never lost," writes Francis, "a deep feeling of pleasure when the nose of an aircraft came up as we were airborne, the satisfaction of nursing an engine to its highest efficiency, or the buoyancy and freedom of the long hours in the sky" (*SQ,* 46).

Back to the Horses

"The war had changed me," Francis writes. After years of being told what to do, how, and when; after years of knowing that death is only a few steps behind; after years of wishing the madness would end; it is no wonder men have trouble adjusting to civilian life, and Dick was no exception. "You can't go home again" might well be a cliché, but it is especially true for war veterans. His father was ready for him to take up where he had left off; with very hard work, George had kept his business intact to pass it on to his son. At first, Dick was glad to take the burden off his father's back, though there clearly was not enough help. Occasionally he got away to ride point-to-points and did poorly at his first public steeplechase at Bangor-on-Dee. He lost his taste for showing: "The change was in me. After six years of an existence when on occasions even life itself was from minute to minute uncertain, the opinion of two men on which of six horses was the best shape seemed to me to be so unimportant as to be ridiculous" (*SQ,* 49). He sought the simpler, more concrete conclusion of a race: the first horse across the line wins. Subtleties of shape and movement, muddled by the possibility of rumor of judges' vanity, greed, or malice, seemed too ephemeral to base meaningful conclusions upon. Francis admits that perhaps he romanticized racing—"in every profession one has to bear public humiliations and private heartaches" (*SQ,* 51)—but what most men want after the endless maybes of military life is a straightforward yes or no, which racing, he imagined, would provide.

He had trouble finding a position. By 1946, he was in his mid-twenties and without experience. His parents had no encouragement for the idea and wanted him to take the safer course of running the family business. He was as tenacious as always, however, and found a trainer who needed his paperwork straightened out. He did a good job as secretary. (In a few of his novels, the hero is engaged in setting a sloppy trainer back on a more businesslike path.) Dick moved in with the family and was given his first amateur mount, Russian Hero, a horse that had never steeplechased before and had taken a few spills in point-to-points. They took an undisgraceful fourth, and Dick began getting many more rides. He was "paying his dues" but doing so impatiently. He was facing a career that might last—if he were lucky—

until he was forty. He studied the courses carefully, walking each before he rode it. He absorbed the tips of other jockeys about the peculiarities of particular tracks and how to get a legal jump on the start, and he learned what dirty tricks experienced jockeys might try on a tyro. He was given a succession of unpromising horses week after week.

Finally, however, he "broke his duck." The jockey scheduled for a favorite, Wrenbury Tiger, was injured, and Dick, after no one else was found, was given his chance. He won. That afternoon he won on another horse. By the end of the season, he had won nine races and moved to halfway up the amateur jockeys' list. On the last day of the season, with his fiancé, Mary, looking on, he was brought literally and figuratively back to earth as he broke his collarbone in a fall—the first of many. In his second season he was given many rides, often on good horses, and the stewards of the National Hunt Committee called him in and demanded he either ride only in amateur races or turn professional immediately. Since amateurs are allowed to ride against professionals in Britain—a concession to the idea of the gentleman sportsman—a too-successful amateur may well be seen as taking food from the mouths of the less fortunate professionals. Like many other people on the verge of their dream, Francis hesitated; he wanted to complete the season as an amateur, and in the back of his mind was the knowledge that there would be no return to the joys of point-to-points or any other amateur races if he failed as a pro. The stewards were adamant, however; he had until the end of the week. In his last amateur race, he again broke his collarbone.

Quest for a Championship

To be a professional jockey, Francis tells us, one must not be swayed by the glamor, one must accept that good luck does not always come to a good rider, and one must not expect to earn a great deal of money because fewer than 10 percent of jockeys holding licenses make a living by racing fees alone (*SQ*, 109–110). He also comments, however, "Surely anyone is a happy man who can spend his life doing what he likes best, and make a career of it" (*SQ*, 101). And happy he was. Besides the riding and winning, there was an enormous amount of driving from meeting to meeting. Francis loved this nomadic existence from 1948 until his retirement in 1957.

His luck and recognizable skill came to the fore almost as soon as he got his license. Lord Bicester, who owned some of the best horses in Britain, hired Francis as his second jockey, to ride when the first jockey, a brilliant Irishman, was engaged elsewhere. For a novice to be in this position was so remarkable that when Dick told his wife, Mary, she thought he was joking. One of his first mounts began inexplicably bleeding from the nostril at the starter's gate, and Francis withdrew it before they began, but in his first outing at the Aintree course in Liverpool, where the Grand National is run, Francis rode Parthenon to a second. To win the Grand National is every jump jockey's dream. The race is difficult, on a challenging course, and is recognized around the world as the premier steeplechase. Francis's first chance came on Parthenon, Lord Bicester's second hope for the race. Almost at the last minute, the Irish jockey was hurt, and Lord Bicester showed his confidence in Francis by placing him on his best horse, Roimond. When the great day arrived, "I thought the nervous excitement I felt before I went out to ride Roimond was because it was my first National, but I felt it every year afterwards. One never gets used to it" (*SQ,* 77).

The story of Dick Francis in the Grand National is one of irony following irony. In his first race, Roimond lost the lead just before the finish to Russian Hero, the first horse Francis had ridden in a competitive steeplechase. Francis had also jockeyed Russian Hero to several victories and had once spent all night walking the horse around to save him from a possibly fatal attack of colic. Moreover, Russian Hero had fallen in three races just before the National. Lord Bicester was happy with the second place—he had never gotten better than a seventh (*SQ,* 77–78)—but if Dick had not accepted his offer to ride the best horses in Britain, he would most likely have been on the winner. Roimond had one other chance in the National with Francis on him, but he fell on the first circuit (*SQ,* 130). In 1951, on one of his favorite horses, Finnure, Francis rode up to the start of the National with tremendous hope. The horse was sharp, had won several races, including at Aintree, and had "an accelerator like a Chrysler."[4] At the first fence, however, eleven of thirty-six horses tumbled, ending the race for their jockeys almost before it had begun. Finnure also twisted his hock and never quite recovered his old form (*SQ,* 133). The ultimate disappointment in the Grand National, the race that is the central symbol for Francis's view of life, was that in which he rode the Queen Mother's horse, Devon Loch, in 1956.

Wrote Francis, "A post-mortem one day may find the words 'Devon Loch' engraved on my heart, so everlasting an impression has that gallant animal made upon it" (*SQ,* 213). Dick first noticed him in

1951 and later rode him and found him delightful. Dismounting, he told the trainer, "I would like to ride this horse in the National some day" (*SQ*, 213). In late 1955, the horse showed such form with Francis in the saddle that the same trainer remarked, "We have just seen the winner of the National in action" (*SQ*, 215). Francis, who had achieved his goal of being champion jockey the previous year, laughed when asked about his chances. He caught himself staring into space with emotional pleasure. He had the feeling something might go wrong as it had with Finnure. Fifteen days before the National, he cracked his collarbone for the ninth time, but strapping it with elastic, he concealed the problem, hoping it would mend itself sufficiently. He tested it in a race five days later and was confident it would be no problem. It was not. He planned his National carefully. With Queen Elizabeth, her mother, and Princess Margaret looking on, the race began. Devon Loch took the huge fences like mere hurdles. He barely missed stumbling over a fallen horse, but he passed horse after horse, and Francis was aware of holding back on a massive reserve of power. With three fences to go, he took the lead and leaped the final one as if it were the first. "In all my life," Francis wrote, "I have never experienced a greater joy than the knowledge I was about to win the National" (*SQ*, 1). It was not to be: "The calamity which overtook us was sudden, terrible, and completely without warning. . . . In one stride he was bounding smoothly along, a poem of controlled motion; in the next, his hind legs stiffened and refused to function. He fell flat on his belly, his legs splayed out sideways and backwards in unnatural angles, and when he stood up he could hardly move" (*SQ*, 1).

Photographs of this event are extraordinary. Devon Loch has assumed such an unnatural position that he almost looks as if he had been shot. Francis threw away his whip in "anger and anguish at the cruelty of fate" and later pressed his head against Devon Loch's neck, forlornly asking "What happened?" (*SQ*, 221–222). Devon Loch could never comment on the numerous theories that were advanced, and none of them mattered in the face of the fact that fifty yards from the finish with a commanding lead, something went wrong. The winner, a horse named E. S. B., finished only a second off the best time in the history of the National, indicating Devon Loch would have shattered the record.[5] Francis would later ride Devon Loch to victory in a couple of other races, and in 1957, after a tendon injury, the horse was retired. Francis that year began to notice that owners were avoiding putting him on unreliable horses for fear of his getting hurt. He too was facing retirement, and he was afraid that his epitaph would describe him as the man who never won the National. Later, however, he appreciated the strange silver lining of Devon Loch's cloud: "The . . . fact is . . . if that other mystery hadn't happened, I might never have written all these other ones."[6] "If it hadn't happened I might never have written a book, so really it was a blessing in disguise."[7]

A New Life

Francis had the choice of most other superb athletes: "retiring before physical deterioration is obvious to all, or clinging on until kicked out" (*SQ*, 233). "You're only good for about ten years," he has said. "That's about all your bones can stand in the way of spills."[8] In his career, he had broken one collarbone six times and the other five times. His nose had been broken five times. Excluding ribs, he had broken twenty-one bones. "You don't count broken ribs," Francis has said. "The pain stops when you warm up."[9] One evening, Lord Abergavenny, who had counseled him before, urged him to "retire at the top" (*SQ*, 235). "I knew he was right," Francis told *Sports Illustrated*, "but I didn't want to believe it. When I left him I walked all through Hyde Park alone; I didn't want to face it. After I retired I kept going to the races and just standing around."[10] Like many of his fictional heroes, he had to choose what sort of life he would lead from then on. But what was he to do? He was not even forty. He was offered jobs as an official judge ("an unheard-of position for an ex-jockey" and some indication of his stature), as a race commentator, and, more fatefully, as the "author" of four or more articles to be ghost-written by the staff of the *Sunday Express*. He took all of these jobs and decided to try writing the articles himself. As Red Smith put it, Francis had fallen "on his head often enough to become a writer."[11] It took him a while to figure out he liked writing, despite the *Sunday Express*'s persistently offering him a full-time job. There must have been amazement in those offices when they discovered that the celebrity whose name they had wished to exploit was more than just another unemployed jock. "I never really decided to be a writer," Francis writes, "I just sort of drifted into it. . . . By the autumn the message had got through to my sluggish brain that I really did like what I was doing and that . . . this was IT" (*SQ*, 238).

Earlier literary agent John Johnson (his mother knew Francis's mother) had approached Francis about doing an autobiography. Devon Loch was still fresh in people's minds, and he thought there would be a market for the book. "They politely suggested I work with a ghost writer," Francis told *Life*. "But when this chap came around and suggested he wanted to move in with us, I wanted none of that. My wife Mary said, 'Why don't you write it? I'll put you right with the punctuation.'"[12] It is easy to see the morality of the man in these refusals to put his name to something he had not himself done. As his heroes are concerned about cheating the public by giving a bad ride, Francis himself, despite facing a much diminished income, did not simply take the money and run, because despite general practice to the contrary, the ghosting would have been a kind of cheating. While he was still a professional jockey, he was not permitted to publish, and he did little on the book. A few months later, however, he was free to do as he liked. It is also easy to see why writing appealed to him. As a jockey, once the race started, he was alone with the horse, doing the best he could to make it perform. As a pilot, he had always preferred flying alone. Writing too is a lonely enterprise. The author faces the paper and is totally responsible for the outcome. The author also enjoys a freedom few other professions allow. Writers can soar and leap in their minds with close to the same exhilaration and intensity one gets from flying or riding.

For all its joys, however, like racing it is hard work. Francis learned his skills doing his autobiography and the series of articles for the *Sunday Express*. He tells us that the autobiography was a good place to start, because, after all, the story is pretty much in your own head and you do not have to research the subject (*SQ*, 237). This remark reveals how important the factual basis is to Dick Francis. He works carefully to avoid the kind of daft detail that many other authors, even the best, are careless with. The most celebrated example is likely the snake, trained with a bowl of milk to respond to a whistle, that climbs down a rope and murders a man in Sir Arthur Conan Doyle's "The Speckled Band." Snakes, even exotic Asian ones, are not interested in milk, cannot hear, and cannot climb down a rope. Yet the story is a classic; the creator of Sherlock Holmes is forgiven everything. Francis's stern sense of realism would never allow him to put finesse over fact. He will not write about any place he has not visited, which, as a bonus, indulges his delight in travel. His usual pattern with novels is to research the subject for six months and then write for six months. It is a demanding schedule.

He credits his newspaper job with having taught him much about the art of writing: "The subeditors loved going through and cutting out unnecessary words. . . . I used to stand there by the side of the subeditor, and it used to annoy me intensely if he could find a word which he could take out which was unnecessary."[13] He also said about his autobiography that if it had been rejected everywhere, "I would have accepted at once that I should forget about writing and do something else" (*SQ*, 238). This commonsense attitude kept him from the kind of egomania that prevents people born with greater talent from ever developing. "You won't get him to say anything pretentious," Mary told an interviewer.[14] He took advice from his editors. He learned the discipline of getting an article done, on time, to the length required. He learned (as in riding) that much hard work can be displaced: an editor cuts the story to his or her liking or an advertisement takes up the space allotted for an article, and the article is killed. He learned the Hemingway lesson of the value of each word—newspapers have no space to indulge fancy writing—and he learned to put aside the idea of writing a masterpiece. Sometimes no rider could make a horse win; sometimes there is no way of making an article much more than adequate before deadline. You finish and look for your next mount; better luck next time.

In December 1957, *The Sport of Queens* was published and sold out in a week. It has been in print since. Francis had discovered that journalism did not pay as well as riding, but his choice to increase his income by then writing a novel seems extraordinarily risky. He could have tried more nonfiction. Later pestered by great jockey Lester Piggott to write his biography, Francis did not want to do it, but he began in 1976 or so to write *A Jockey's Life*.[15] The book was interesting to anyone already deeply involved in the subject but only intermittently so to readers who did not already appreciate the glory of Piggott's riding (often the case with sports biographies). Nonetheless Francis could have quickly capitalized on the success of *The Sport of Queens* but instead took a chance on fiction. Mary, he says, suggested it,[16] but his sole inspiration was "the threadbare state of the carpet and a rattle in the car" (*SQ*, 239) or his sons needing educating.[17] He thought a novel might bring in a little money. Why a novel? He had to know that his own status as a celebrity, which had contributed to making his autobiography a success, might serve him not so well in a novel—even one about racing. The judgment of whether a book succeeds or fails is also much more akin to the judgments of horse showing than the clearcut ending of a race. Yet as he had also found writing an amiable occupation, he would also be freer in writing a novel. As he reveals in *Forfeit,* a number of aspects of journalism leave a bitter aftertaste for him. He nonetheless endured them for sixteen years, giving up his column only in 1973. Most of those elements (shown in his fiction) would be absent or lessened appreciably in writing a novel.

"Writing a novel," he tells us, "proved to be the hardest, most self-analysing task I had ever attempted, far worse than an autobiography, and its rewards were greater than I expected" (*SQ,* 239). *Dead Cert* was published in January 1962, and its immediate success guaranteed Francis's second career. He received a £300 advance, but the book went on to earn much more.[18] He had gone professional again in a profession most people would think had little relation to horse racing. His subject was the track, and because he had always liked mystery thrillers, he employed that basic form, modifying it to suit his preferences. Like Athena springing fully armed from the brow of Zeus, *Dead Cert* set up from the beginning a Francis formula that he would employ past two decades of steady writing at a book-a-year clip, varying it only occasionally and slightly.

The success was immediate and soon very lucrative, with subsequent books more than taking care of education, carpet, and car. He won a Silver Dagger from the British Crime Writers Association for *For Kicks* in 1965 and then an Edgar Allan Poe Award of the Mystery Writers of America for best mystery with *Forfeit* in 1970. *Whip Hand* took the best mystery awards in both Britain and the United States and gave him his first appearance on the *New York Times* best-seller list. Changing American publishers in 1980 resulted in his being marketed as a best-seller rather than a mystery author, and it resulted in *Reflex's* selling 85,000 hardback copies, becoming a Book-of-the-Month Club selection, and a $400,000 paperback rights sale. Overall Francis has sold about twenty-five million copies, and all of his books are in print.[19] He has been translated into nearly two dozen foreign languages. There are so many foreign editions he no longer has room for them at home and donates the copies to the Seaman's Home.[20] Each year his new novel shoots up the best-seller list; more amazingly, their critical reception is usually, at the very least, kind. Reviewers who build their reputations on lacerating authors may occasionally complain about this or that, but it is extremely difficult to find an outright negative review.

Although his stories are highly visual—what could be more spectacular than horses vaulting fences?—Francis has not had notable success in film. *Dead Cert* was filmed in Britain but did poorly at the box office. On television, however, "The Racing Game," a series of Sid Halley stories, was filmed for Yorkshire Television and later aired in the United States on PBS's *Mystery!* in 1979–80. These resulted in an upsurge of interest in his novels and a corresponding rise in sales. Francis also discovered on a visit to the Soviet Union that Soviet television had adapted *Dead Cert* quite successfully. In his champion season as a jockey, Francis rode 76 winners in 331 races. With novels he has had 26 winners so far, but the track is always far more crowded and filled with many more hurdles and fences than any course he ever faced.

Writing

Francis comments in his autobiography: "The process of producing fiction is a mystery which I still do not understand. Indeed, as the years go by I understand it less and less, and I am constantly afraid that one day I will lose the knack of it and produce discord, like a pianist forgetting where to find middle C" (*SQ,* 240). He then romantically goes on to meditate that the books write themselves—in a sense, that it is impossible for him to produce anything other than what he produces: "Books write authors as much as authors write books" (*SQ,* 240). "It doesn't do to analyze something like a glass of champagne or a good story idea. . . . You just accept it and know it is going to make you feel better about things."[21] He has also told interviewers that he hangs about racetracks until he gets an idea; the connections that turn an overheard bit of conversation, the look on a jockey's face, the gait of a horse's walk into the plot of a novel are part of the magic of the creative process. As Sir Kenneth Clark said of J. M. W. Turner's inspiration, this "shows us how far we are from understanding the nature of genius."[22]

Research is an important part of Francis's writing. His knowledge of the world of horses is so broad that it is always the base on which he builds his mysteries. No one else has conveyed the feeling of riding more evocatively than he has. No one else can recreate the smells, sounds, and atmosphere of stables and racetracks. Knowing so much about the effect of violence upon his own body translates into some of the most excruciating, though never gratuitous, scenes of torture ever written—no small matter in a time in which violence is the staple dish offered by television and motion pictures. Yet Francis has remained popular by never quite allowing himself to be predictable. His heroes are not all jockeys. Some, in fact, are quite ignorant of racing when they come into contact with it. In his gallery of heroes, there are many different occupations, and that is where the research comes in. For settings, he has become quite a globe-trotter in picking up local color for his novels. He has been to the Soviet Union, Australia, and South Africa, and he once took a three-week Greyhound bus trip across the United States for *Blood Sport,* with an agonizing forty-two-hour Denver-to-New York stint.[23]

At his best, this research is so integrated into the novel that he avoids the mistake of many less talented authors who seem intent on putting in all the information they collect, even if it is not relevant. It never makes sense in books for someone in a particular occupation to explain something in detail that he or she would take for granted. A jockey, for example, would not explain to a trainer what the withers are or a pilot engage in a long lesson about the Bernoulli principle. Francis usually manages, however, to convey information without making readers aware that he is explaining. There is much arcana in the world of horses and the other professions he chooses to write about, but it is gently revealed. John Leonard wrote in the *New York Times,* "I am entirely innocent of race tracks. And yet: Not to read Dick Francis because you don't like horses is like not reading Dostoyevsky because you don't like God."[24] When explanations are needed, Francis resorts to naive onlookers; someone will ask what the withers are or how an airplane stays aloft. Only occasionally does the illusion slip when a character explains too much. The anonymous sources of *The Danger* acknowledged in the book's dedication undoubtedly provided many details about kidnapping, but too many of them diminish the pleasure. Matt Shore of *Rat Race* also explains more about flying than is needed. Usually, however, Francis strongly identifies with his narrator and takes for granted what the hero would take for granted. This makes his characters much more credible. They imply a wealth of knowledge they do not reveal.

Francis has also always strongly credited his wife, Mary, for contributing to the books. "We discuss the plots, we write as a team really," Francis has said.[25] She has a degree in English and French from London University.[26] She gets deeply into the research, she watches the punctuation and spelling, and she suggests better phrasings. In the six months they research the books, she travels with her husband, much as she accompanied him to all the races she could when he was a jockey. He told the *New Yorker* that on the long drives, they think about plots.

"Mary is very helpful to me. . . . She also works out a lot of the crimes for the novels. My colleagues say she has a crooked mind."[27] In *The Sport of Queens,* he tells how Mary first became part of his research process. He needed information on gemstones, the hobby of the villain in *Odds Against.* She found out about them in Oxford's public library. Later, for *Flying Finish,* she flew with Dick in a horse transport to Italy, taking notes and photographs. When his newspaper work would have interfered with new flying lessons to research *Rat Race,* Mary took them instead, pursuing the course to the end and becoming a licensed pilot (*SQ,* 245). She has even written a beginner's guide to flying that has been placed in the Royal Air Force library.[28] She learned oil painting during the writing of *In the Frame* and photography during *Reflex* (many of the published photographs of Dick are by her). She tried writing computer programs during *Twice Shy.* She went down into a gold mine for *Smokescreen* and up into a hot-air balloon with Dick for *Whip Hand* (*SQ,* 245–46).

This remarkable relationship goes far beyond research, of course. Dick met Mary at a wedding in 1945. Even before she spoke, he fell immediately in love. Part the yearning of a war veteran for a normal life, part magic, this "unreasonable way to choose a companion for life," as he put it (*SQ,* 47), was some of the best luck he ever had and perhaps salved much of the despair of his bad luck. She visited every couple of weeks while Dick worked at his father's stables. "My courtship," she would joke, "was spent leaning over the bottom half of stable doors while Dick mucked out an endless row of horses" (*SQ,* 49). They had to conceal their relationship from Mary's grandfather, a clergyman who, like many Francis characters indifferent to racing, was soon converted to following Dick's career gleefully.[29] As the daughter of the owner of a printing factory, she knew little about horses, and their families thought her lack of interest would doom the marriage. Mary once said, "His family thought it was ridiculous him marrying a girl who couldn't help him with horses."[30] No other family has ever been more wrong. "From the first," wrote Dick, "it was a joke between us, and through the years we have found it has balanced my own single-minded concentration into a shared sense of proportion" (*SQ,* 86).

They were living in a hayloft flat when their first crisis occurred. Mary went to London to spend a few days with her mother and came down with infantile paralysis. When she called to tell Dick, she sounded almost cheerful and insisted he do his races that day before coming.

She was seriously ill, however, and was placed in an iron lung. When he tried to tell his mother on the telephone, he uncontrollably wept. Mary, a stiff-upper-lip Britisher herself, insisted he go on racing, however, saying that she was all right, despite all the evidence to the contrary. It was almost a relief for Dick when broken bones allowed him two weeks to sit by Mary doing crossword puzzles with her. Their first son was born before she had recovered full strength, and the harrowing experience of her illness became translated into the powerful emotions of *Forfeit*.

Also sympathetic to the jockey's wife's lot—watching on the rails, waiting for the inevitable falls that could mean anything from a bruise to a broken neck to death—he appreciates her for always sticking with him in those years. A jockey's wife cheers happily when her husband wins, Francis comments, but always knows that the bad falls are coming, "like kings disastrously turning up in a game of clock patience" (*SQ*, 86). "I think it's worse for them, much worse than for the jockeys," he told John C. Carr.[31] Yet Mary's support was always with him, even when she faced permanent paralysis. When he describes the typical day of a jockey's life, it contains kissing the children good-bye and going off to the races with her (*SQ*, 115). When he delights in his trip to ride in the International Steeplechase at Belmont Park, he shows how much he enjoyed sharing the trip with her (*SQ*, 202–12). After his unfortunate ride on Devon Loch in the Grand National, some of his depression was lifted by a walk by the River Dee with Mary, and he tells us how she spent that night as sleepless as he (*SQ*, 223). Is it any wonder that with such a warm partnership in his life that Francis is praised for his portrayals of stable, intelligent women?

As to the mechanics of writing, Francis tries to begin a novel each January and finish it by April 30.[32] He composes in longhand with a pencil in a school exercise book (*SQ*, 241). Every day he exercises and then puts in five or six hours at writing.[33] He often writes at night or rises early and writes until 7:30, when he rides at a neighbor's farm.[34] He goes slowly, sentence by sentence, sure of what he wants to say in one line before moving on to the next. If he likes what he has written the previous day, he goes on; if he does not like it, he rarely discards it, but rather modifies a few words or maybe adds a sentence. When he has a couple of chapters written, he puts the work on the word processor. Thus he continues to the end. Wholesale changes are never any good for Francis. Even his publisher is resigned to the fact that he produces something worse when forced to make large changes. There are no second and third drafts for Dick Francis (*SQ*, 241). It's once over the hurdles and lean your nose toward the finish. You do your best, take what fate dishes out, and don't complain. There are usually no second chances on the important things.

Chapter Two

The Reluctant Detective

The Hard-Boiled Mystery

The term *mystery* seems simple enough. We all seem to know what it means in some general sense: a piece of fiction containing a crime and its investigation. Yet to define the term precisely is impossible. Usually the crime is murder, simply because it is difficult to get as interested in lesser crimes. Usually there is a single detective (often with a less clever assistant), either professional or amateur, who works through a succession of clues to unmask the criminal. But writers can depart from the preestablished pattern and can cause a redefinition of *mystery* each time the term is used. By analogy, *mystery* is like *race*. The racial categories anthropologists have used for some time are more fluid than most people recognize. There is within any of the races—Negroid, Mongoloid, Caucasoid, Australoid—more variation among individuals of the race than among the races themselves. The genre of the mystery similarly includes works as diverse as Agatha Christie's *Ten Little Indians*, Mickey Spillane's *I, The Jury*, John D. MacDonald's *Cinnamon Skin*, Stanislaw Lem's *The Investigation*, and Mario Vargas Llosa's *Who Killed Palomino Molero?* and in many instances mysteries are more different from each other than they are from nonmysteries. It is possible to argue that Feodor Dostoyevsky's *Crime and Punishment* is a mystery, or *Hamlet*, yet the reader who enters a store and asks a clerk for a mystery is not directed to Russian classics or Shakespeare.

The mystery is usually divided into two imprecise categories imprecisely dubbed the "British" mystery and the "hard-boiled" (or "American") detective novel. Each is recognizable as being distinct, although the particular features of individual novels may blur the categories. The British mystery is typically an intellectual game based around tricky plotting. The author presents a series of clues, some relevant and some not, while revealing the personalities of a series of suspects. Usually the clues point in various directions to different suspects, and by the final chapter, optimally, only the most rigorous logic and careful interpretation of the clues by the erudite, cultured, and intelligent detective narrows the suspects. The reader's role is to outguess the detective, and the reader's delight comes from the intricacy of the criminal puzzle. Standard features in the British mystery are a limited number of suspects in an hermetic environment such as a country house, a train, or a ship. The police, if available, are usually unintelligent clods who rush in to arrest the wrong person. Despite the subject, British mysteries are frequently humorous as the intellectuality of the puzzle overwhelms the seriousness of the crime. A certain detachment ensues in which the characters become pawns in the problem. Like Colonel Mustard and Miss Scarlet in the game *Clue,* the suspects do not often draw much sympathy. They are removed from the playing board often without a sense of human loss or continue as unidimensional characters. The emphasis in the British mystery is on form and mental gymnastics. A poorly done British mystery suffers from a lack of realism. In a well-done one, the characters can be engaging, satirical, and occasionally realistic. Typical British detectives are Sherlock Holmes, Jane Marple, Hercule Poirot, Adam Dalgleish, and, on this side of the ocean, Charlie Chan, the television incarnation of Perry Mason, and Philo Vance.

The hard-boiled novel, in contrast, seemed extraordinarily realistic during its rise during the 1920s and 1930s, though now it has become such a pattern that it often seems antiquated. Its patent appeal to macho values has become particularly awkward. "Hard-boiled" in American slang has meant "insensitive," "unfeeling," and "callous." The world of these novels is harsh, corrupt, and filled with injustices that can be remedied only partly. The tone is tough, the message often ironic. The detective succeeds as often by bulldog perseverance as by wit. His body usually suffers more strain than his brain. The setting is usually urban, and the city is filled with potential suspects. The characters are often streetwise people on the lower rungs of the economic ladder: prostitutes, newsboys, petty thugs, and gangsters. The criminals are not as clever as they are dangerous, preferring force to trickery, brutality to slyness. Like the British mystery, it is an easy form to parody, particularly in its terse, often exaggerated, language, influenced in no small measure by the austere style of Ernest Hemingway. Refinement and sophistication are usually sneered at as being masks for effeminacy, weakness, or duplicity. At their worst, hard-boiled novels consist of a succession of brutalities and titillations, all threaded on a thin plot, the impulse to realism disappearing behind sexual obsessions with overheated women and brutal beatings. At their best, they tell us something about how to live in an imperfect world; they are almost existential in their message that acting with honor is what makes a man—not success, love, or physical attractiveness. Typical hard-boiled detectives include Sam Spade, the Continental Op, Philip Marlowe, Jake Gittes of the film *Chinatown,* and Mike Hammer.

Note, however, how often it is necessary to employ *usually* in describing these forms. A precise definition is possible only when the cross-overs are ignored. It is easy to forget that Philip Marlowe, the paradigm for dozens of hard-boiled detectives, amuses himself by playing chess, something often missing in movies based on Chandler's novels, probably because it is difficult to justify against the lack of sympathy for refinement. It is also easy to overlook the fact that quintessential British detective Sherlock Holmes often enters the underground world of London in disguise and accumulates evidence in a manner not demonstrably different from that of Dashiell Hammett's Continental Op. In the arts, as in reality, categorizations can be useful, despite the frequency with which they may stub their toes on specific details. Keeping these imprecisions in mind is important in discussing a writer who works within these categories, as Dick Francis does.

Francis writes hard-boiled detective novels, but no one should expect that to provide an absolute explanation of what he does. (He himself has said that he does not think of himself as a "mystery" or a "detective" novelist but as an "adventure" novelist.)[1] Nor should such a statement be considered to provide an explanation of his success as a popular novelist. Although readers have relatively clear expectations of a hard-boiled mystery as compared to a literary novel, it is the variations within the formula that provide the interest. Dick Francis has developed his own variations to the hard-boiled detective novel, variations that recur throughout his work and that have, after more than twenty novels, created a "Francis formula." A reader of a Francis novel has certain expectations; Francis, an extraordinary native talent, has become a worldwide success by feeding those reader expectations without becoming tediously repetitive.

Alan York

One of the major affinities Francis has with the hard-boiled detective novel is in his portrayal of the main character. Francis has remarked: "My heroes *are* all very similar. They are the sort of chaps I'd like to meet. I build a character up out of a number of people. Sometimes

I'd like to think I was as good as the heroes I create, but I'm not. I do like to write about good types. Probably my dark men, or bad characters, aren't bad enough. My heroes are all male. I can't really place myself in a woman's mind."[2] The heroes become clearly recognizable as the British cousins of Sam Spade, Philip Marlowe, and Lew Archer. The blueprint for them appears in Raymond Chandler's often-quoted essay, "The Simple Art of Murder."[3] Comparing a typical Francis hero with the man described at the end of Chandler's essay makes the connections obvious. Chandler writes:

Down these mean streets a man must go who is not himself mean, who is neither tarnished nor afraid. . . . He must be a complete man and a common man and yet an unusual man. He must be, to use a rather weathered phrase, a man of honor—by instinct, by inevitability, without thought of it, and certainly without saying it. He must be the best man in his world and a good enough man for any world. I do not care much about his private life; he is neither a eunuch nor a satyr; I think he might seduce a duchess and I am quite sure he would not spoil a virgin; if he is a man of honor in one thing, he is that in all things.

He is a relatively poor man, or he would not be a detective at all. He is a common man or he could not go among common people. He has a sense of character, or he would not know his job. He will take no man's money dishonestly and no man's insolence without a due and dispassionate revenge. He is a lonely man and his pride is that you will treat him as a proud man or be very sorry you ever saw him. He talks as a man of his age talks—that is, with rude wit, a lively sense of the grotesque, a disgust for sham, and a contempt for pettiness.

The story is this man's adventure in search of a hidden truth, and it would be no adventure if it did not happen to a man fit for adventure. He has a range of awareness that startles you, but it belongs to him by right, because it belongs to the world he lives in. If there were enough like him, the world would be a very safe place to live in, without becoming too dull to be worth living in.[4]

Although there are variations to the Chandler formula, Francis's first novel, *Dead Cert,* adheres closely to it. The narrator and hero is Alan York, an amateur steeplechaser from Rhodesia. York, like most other Francis heroes, much more resembles Chandler's hero than differs from him. In this first novel, the Francis hero is already nearly fully developed into the man who will appear in all the successive novels, with most of their traits parallel to those described by Chandler. The "mean streets" a Francis hero must go down is usually the world of horse racing, and York's behavior in the corruption of that world is typical of later heroes: he cannot be bought. He will not fix a race or cheat the horse's owner, even under physical threat to himself. The jockeys Sandy Mason and Joe Nantwich prove that corruption, out of simple greed or financial stress, is unremarkable in racing (though "rare" because jockeys might lose their licenses[5]), and although York himself maintains his integrity, he is not harsh in judging those who do not. He makes no effort to call down the authorities on jockeys who have been corrupted, which is reminiscent of the indulgence or pity hard-boiled detectives commonly have toward bookmakers, safecrackers, and other petty criminals, and also of the hard-boiled trait of righting wrongs on their own.

York does not need to race. His father is wealthy, and he rides out of enjoyment. That he finds the act of charging a horse over fences his main source of entertainment is a good indication of York's physical courage, but if a reader should want to take that for granted—other jockeys are revealed to be cowardly on and off their horses—there are scenes such as those when York is dragged inside a horse box and confronted by three hooligans who warn him "to lay off asking questions about [the murdered] Major Davidson." At first, however, York thinks he is going to be kidnapped and ransomed. Despite being held by both arms, with a knife at his chest, York resists. "I was sure," says York, with hard-boiled sangfroid, "that this little melodrama was intended to soften me up into a suitable frightened state of mind." Whatever its intention, York is not softened. He pretends to sag in fear so that the thugs relax; then he springs forward into the knife, kicking the knife wielder in the groin. The escape fails, and they punish him, eventually tossing him to the road from out of the moving horse box (DC, 71–77). Later York recounts the event to Inspector Lodge, who is investigating Davidson's murder. Why, Lodge asks, would a man with a knife held at his chest spring forward? "I wouldn't have been so keen if he'd held the point a bit higher up" says York; "but it was against my breastbone. You'd need a hammer to get a knife through that. I reckoned that I'd knock it out of Sonny's hand rather than into me" (81). This act tells a reader more about the kind of stuff Alan York is made of than anything Francis could have written. Anyone who would knock a knife out of a killer's hand with his chest is going to take more than one criminal organization to bring him down—especially when it is the possibility of York's being ransomed by his father that provokes this wild act. "I would never be able to live it down" (74), he says, frightened more by his potential embarrassment than by the death or mutilation facing him.

York's honor extends into his private life and corresponds also to Chandler's remarks. Francis's heroes are never eunuchs—they are interested in sex—but they are never satyrs, bedding only women they love and declining casual offers. Francis heroes never victimize women, either through brutality or sexual affairs, adopting a chivalrous attitude suitable to the "knightly" quality that both Chandler and he create. In *Dead Cert,* the interesting tension between York and Scilla Davidson is an example. York has been living in the Davidson home, and when his best friend, Bill, is tripped by a wire across the racetrack and killed, he offers to leave so that Scilla will not be the victim of gossip. Inspector Lodge has implied that because York was riding behind Bill, he might have known about the wire and, living in such proximity to Scilla, might have a motive to want Bill dead. She, however, is on the verge of collapse from the shock of Bill's death. "I don't care what anyone says," she pleads. "I need you here. Please, please, don't go away." Later they go to their separate beds. He is awakened at 2 A.M. when she comes into his room and turns on the bedside table: "She looked ridiculously young and defenceless. She was wearing a pale blue knee-length chiffon nightdress which flowed transparently about her slender body and fell like mist over her small breasts" (64). The attraction York has hinted at in previous chapters but denied is obvious, and he runs his fingers through her hair; however, he goes no further. He wraps her in an eiderdown quilt and talks to her about unimportant matters until she, after weeping, falls asleep. After she stops twisting and turning in sleep, York carries her back to her own room so that she will not suffer any shame. York would never take advantage of an emotionally upset woman drugged with sleeping pills regardless of his attraction for her. As Chandler writes, "[If] he is a man of honor in one thing, he is that in all things." Yet toward the end of the scene, he confesses that he "should not have been content to be so passive a bedfellow had I held Kate in my arms instead" (66).

Kate Ellery-Penn is York's only romance in the novel. The wordiness suggests, however, the embarrassment of admitting the desire, which gives York the charm of a red-faced adolescent trying to admit his sexual feelings in order to prove he is a man. It would not do for readers to think York is not interested in that sort of diversion, but he also should not be too lustful. Besides damaging the hero's uprightness, explicit sex scenes are rare in mysteries, and Francis is suitably circumspect in this regard. Notably absent also is York's explanation of his behavior, perhaps because it might constitute trendy boasting about his sensitivity or how it is possible to have friendship between the sexes. A man of honor does not brag. Even when he could score a coup against his rival for Kate's attention by letting his family wealth be known, he allows Kate's Edwardian aunt to go on thinking he is merely a jockey. Later in the novel, as he continues his courtship, he is clear about his physical attraction to Kate, saying he would like to "throw her in the car and drive off to some wild and lonely hollow . . . for a purpose of which the cave men would thoroughly have approved" (*DC,* 136). Kate, however, is rather reserved, and York does not force himself on her, resulting in her ultimately agreeing to marry him despite his causing the death of her uncle.

There is, in the traditional hard-boiled novel, a clear implication that money taints anyone who has it. The hero is frequently tested by offers of money that he either refuses or accepts only to pass it on to the grieving widow, dispossessed family, or some other victim. (Philip Marlowe, for example, gives the "Madison" to Terry in the last chapter of *The Long Goodbye* and scoffs at the enormous bribe offers at the end of *The Big Sleep.*) Chandler describes his hero as being a relatively poor man, or he would not be a detective. This is one way that Francis has changed the hard-boiled formula. Money does not taint his main characters, as it does not taint Marlowe and other hard-boiled detectives, but a Francis hero frequently has plenty of money. The character has solid values that lead him in search of hidden truth even when the danger makes it unwise to do so. Mere possession of wealth is not sufficient to corrupt. When Chandler says that the detective must be a common man or he could not go among common people, Francis also adjusts this aspect of the formula by making his frequently wealthy protagonists able to reach across divisions of class and wealth: to go among common people because the fundamental values (courage, integrity, perseverance) at any level of wealth are recognized in any class. Furthermore the connection between being poor and being a detective is destroyed in Francis's novels; only one of his heroes is a private investigator—Sid Halley of *Whip Hand*—and only one is a professional investigator—David Cleveland of *Slayride.* Alan York is an "amateur" jockey in the original sense of the word; he rides for the love of it. He investigates only because he is forced to by his sense of duty and imminent threat.

The Francis formula therefore follows Chandler's statement that the hero must be a "complete man and a common man and yet an unusual man." Money, however, does not determine whether a man or woman is petty or deceptive, evil or corrupt. In fact, Francis repeats the pattern of many of the stories used in Alfred Hitchcock's best films, such as *North by Northwest, The Thirty-Nine Steps,* and *The Man Who Knew Too Much.* A person, nice but ostensibly ordinary, is thrust into a dangerous situation, which then reveals exactly how resourceful and extraordinary this person is.

The beginning of *Dead Cert* is very much in this vein. Riding in a February race at Maidenhead, York is trailing the prerace favorite, Admiral, ridden by his friend: "All, in fact, was going as expected. Bill Davidson was about to win his ninety-seventh steeplechase" (7). Suddenly, however, Admiral falls, in a particularly unnatural way (killing Bill in the process) that arouses York's suspicions. After the race, he finds a wire that has been stretched across the course, and it becomes obvious that his friend, riding a "dead cert" (an absolute certainty to win), has been murdered. Typical also of this type of mystery beginning is the fact that York has no evidence that the police feel is adequate to pursue, and York finds himself thrust into the role of detective, partly because he is a suspect, curiously, in a crime that would be unknown were it not for him, but mostly because his early inquiries set him up as a possible next victim. There may be a grudging respect between the police and the detective in a hard-boiled novel, and there may even be amiability, as there is between Inspector Lodge and York, but the police are utterly ineffective until the hero delivers the evildoers.

Dead Cert therefore adheres rather closely to the hard-boiled formula described by Chandler and exemplified by his and Hammett's novels. Francis varies the formula only enough to make it distinctive as his own by expressing certain personal sensibilities in his attitude toward women and police, for example, and in the character of his hero.

After *Dead Cert,* Francis added a few other aspects to his fiction that mitigated the general machismo of the hard-boiled novel with such elements as the emotional scarring of the hero in his family life, but he has never wandered too far from his pattern. Generally he is most successful when he clings to that pattern and least interesting when he does not. The recipe can be ruined by poor-quality ingredients or by leaving something out, but the dish is familiar year after year. This is not a criticism. Structural repetition is an important ingredient in the mystery genre—one of its guilty pleasures for sophisticated readers.

Sid Halley

Francis's most popular hero to date is ex-jockey Sid Halley, who appears in *Odds Against* and *Whip Hand*. The latter novel, appearing fourteen years after the first, is dedicated to Mike Gwilym and Jacky Stoller, who, as actor and producer, respectively, brought Sid Halley to television. Broadcast in the United States on the PBS series *Mystery!*, "The Racing Game" gave an excellent rendition of Halley. Gwilym is a talented actor who has also been seen in the United States in motion pictures and in the title role of the BBC production of Shakespeare's *Pericles,* among others. Francis himself particularly approved of Gwilym: "The first time he came he just walked in and it was just as if Sid Halley were sitting down and having a drink with us. I was delighted with the way he played the part. He'd never ridden—had to take riding lessons."[6]

In most respects, Halley fits the pattern of a typical Francis hero, although he is also unusual in two major respects. First, he is one of only two heroes Francis has repeated. Second, he is a detective. For most of Francis's career, Halley was the only main character Francis had used more than once in a novel, although recently, in *Break In* and *Bolt,* he has reprised the character of Christmas "Kit" Fielding. Generally mystery writers have refined their protagonist detectives and repeated them over the years. Perhaps because of the necessity of writing so much, so rapidly, the burden of creating an intriguing detective each time out is merely adding an additional burden to the already formidable tasks of plotting, characterizing suspects, and so on. Francis, however, is primarily interested in creating main characters, he has said, "learning something about the world in which the main character lives."[7] Repeating a protagonist also has the liability of stabilizing a character; much change from novel to novel might confuse readers who do not read them sequentially. Realism eventually suffers in these series because of the difficulty of making the character age or develop in any substantial way. Also, it frequently leads to the unlikely and unintentional whimsy that every time certain detectives take a holiday, a corpse drops into their lives. This is a pattern in mysteries that is particularly amenable to television. It is extraordinary that viewers are willing to accept, each Sunday, that Jessica Fletcher of CBS's "Murder She Wrote" will step out of a taxi and into a killing, often multiple. It is even more extraordinary that the people whom she visits do not flee at the sight of her. She carries death in her luggage like other women carry extra nylons. Yet Mrs. Fletcher is quite routine in the world of the mystery, and viewers come to hold a deep affection for her genial sameness just as readers develop a taste for the traits of Sherlock Holmes, Hercule Poirot, Nero Wolfe, or Maigret. Such characters are a part of the comforting stability of mystery fiction—a lovable stability in this unpredictable world.

Francis, however, has assiduously avoided repeating his protagonist, with the sole exceptions of Sid Halley and Kit Fielding, because, he once said, he does not consider himself a full-blown novelist and painting the main character helps him to fill up the book.[8] If this is true, then the impulse serves him well, if only for his straightforward pursuit of realism. Francis's heroes are rarely detectives, and common sense does not permit pilots, jockeys, bankers, antique dealers, wine merchants, and others to spend their lives stumbling into a succession of criminal webs. The events in which they find themselves involved are meant to be unusual, and it is utterly unrealistic for such catastrophes to happen to the same person more than once. Francis's heroes usually do not wish to play detective; they are forced into the role because of loyalty to a person or because it is the only way to eliminate a threat. Instead of being drawn in, a detective may be asked as part of his job to stick his nose into a crime (*Whip Hand* begins this way), though private investigators rarely do much that would make interesting reading, spending most of their time looking for runaways, wayward spouses, and light-fingered clerks. (Few private eyes have the financial option of saying "I don't do divorce" as they so often do in novels.) Realistically only the police are likely to deal with a succession of crimes, the vast majority of those numbingly uninteresting.

Francis apparently was frequently asked if he would do a third Sid Halley book, but he told the *Washington Post,* "Not being a born writer, I find building up my main characters as I go helps me to fill up the books. If I started with a ready-made character like Sid, I should be lost. I won't say Sid Halley will never come back again, although I'm getting old now. Can't go on writing."[9] These remarks are notable for the practical, unpretentious, professional attitude Francis takes to writing and because they show how central his main character is to the book. The protagonist is more important than the actual mystery. That the puzzle is always secondary is apparent in Francis's best novels.[10]

Halley, because he is an investigator, might be expected to be thrust into criminal investigations in a way not much different from Marlowe,

Holmes, or any of the other detective heroes: a person comes into the
office needing help in something perhaps unusual but often mundane.
The situation elaborates into murder and mystery. But when Francis
introduced Halley in *Odds Against,* he departed from this obvious
pattern. As the novel opens, the ex-jockey is a detective in name only.
Employed by an eminent firm of investigators, Hunt Radnor, he is in
the situation of so many other famous ex-athletes, seemingly being
exploited for his name. Hunt Radnor has a successful Racing Section,
and a former champion jockey on staff would be good for picking up
clients. Halley himself suspects that "somewhere in the background
. . . my father-in-law was pulling strings,"[11] although later his father-
in-law tells him that he had nothing significant to do with Halley's
being offered the job. Radnor had independently decided that a man
with a champion jockey's character—he had seen Halley race—was the
"sort of chap" he needed to take over the business when age caught
up with him (652). At the agency, Halley is not expected to do much
other than pick up his check, at least while Radnor tolerates him.
Halley remarks: "Radnor's two unvarying excuses for giving me nothing
to do were first that I was too well known to the whole racing world
to be inconspicuous, and second, that even if I didn't seem to care,
he was not going to be the one to give an ex-champion jockey tasks
which meant a great loss of face. . . . As a result, I spent most of
my time kicking around the office reading other people's reports"
(449–50). No one seems to mind this arrangement except Halley, who
interprets it as a reflection against his manhood, a reflection he masochistically accepts because he feels he deserves it: "Perhaps they
[Radnor's staff] realized, as I did, that my employment was an act of
pity. Perhaps they thought I should be too proud to accept that sort
of pity. I wasn't" (448).

Halley, therefore, like the typical Francis hero, is not a detective
when *Odds Against* opens. He has, it is true, been shot while confronting
a burglar, but he admits that he would not have been shot if he hadn't
been "careless because bored" (445). He was not doing even that
simple job well because he was not taking it seriously. He has been
unprofessional, one of the greatest sins in Francis's novels. How Halley
redeems himself, rising above his despair at having lost his racing career,
is an important parallel to the mystery plot. Halley may not be a
detective when the book begins, but he becomes one as the book
progresses. At first he is willing to wallow in self-pity at his crippled
hand and lost career and to accept the pity of others. As he lies in

the hospital bed, he says, "I had the impression that he [Radnor] was waiting for something, but if it wasn't for me to leave, I didn't know what" (450). The answer is apparent: Radnor had seen the stuff of which Halley was made. A man like that, even after the loss of his career and use of his hand, could never end up wasting the rest of his life. Radnor is waiting for the time when Halley will become a professional. By the end of the novel, it is, ironically, Radnor himself who needs Halley to kick him out of depression and into action as Radnor blames himself for Halley's losing the rest of his hand (648–52).

Most other aspects of Halley's character are typical of Francis's protagonists. They are deeply scarred emotionally or physically, or both. Halley had gotten used to dozens of falls from horses (falls that Francis himself has had intimate experience with), but the fall that ended his career mutilated his left hand. He describes the accident in the following way: " 'Oh, an accident. A sharp bit of metal.' A razor-sharp racing horseshoe attached to the foot of a horse galloping at thirty miles an hour, to be exact. A hard kicking slash as I rolled on the ground from an easy fall. One of those things. . . . I'd really known at once when I saw my stripped wrist, with the blood spurting out in a jet and the broken bones showing white, that I was finished as a jockey" (542–43). The surgeons wanted to amputate the hand immediately, but Halley, denying the inevitable, insisted on their doing what repairs they could. After two painful and futile attempts, they refused to go on, and Halley was left with a twisted and useless hand.

This inability to confront the reality of his loss is a much deeper problem than the mutilation itself, and Halley is a typical Francis hero in having emotional scars.[12] Francis heroes are not men of iron who shed unhappiness easily. They are not impervious to psychic trauma. They feel fear, paralyzing self-doubt, profound guilt, or deep loss. Parallel to and more important to Francis's way of thinking than the crime plot is the plot of self-discovery or self-acceptance. By novel's end, the hero not only knows himself better but has come to a reconciliation with his past. Perhaps this contributes to Francis's not generally repeating his heroes; it is unrealistic that any individual would likely have a succession of emotional crises of great weight (without their ultimately being trivialized), thereby eliminating in Francis's gallery of heroes the intellectual, unruffled detective of so many mysteries by other authors. The effect of providing more than one catastrophic emotional crisis in a lifetime may be seen in *Whip Hand,* the second

Halley novel; Francis seems to stretch himself a bit in devising Halley's confrontation with fear, though he makes it generally plausible.

Throughout *Odds Against,* Halley's crippled hand is shown to be the source of his spiritual paralysis. It is obviously why he is willing to accept what he perceives as Radnor's pity. He mentions the humiliation of asking people to cut his meat for him, and he tries to keep the hand concealed in his pocket. One of the most horrifying scenes in the novel occurs early on, when the villainous Howard and Doria Kraye determine to humiliate Halley by pulling the hand out. The psychic violence of the scene leaves no doubt what kind of people the Krayes are, and Halley's desperate struggle to prevent their sadistic humiliation reveals the extent of the psychic trauma. When Doria suggests to her husband that they punish Halley in this way, he shows how much he would hate it. He squirms and struggles until he is nauseated and cannot resist further: "They looked steadily at the wasted, flabby, twisted hand, and at the scars on my forearm, wrist and palm, not only the terrible jagged marks of the original injury but the several tidier ones of the operations since. It was a mess, a right and proper mess" (493). Doria screws up her face in distaste, and Howard cruelly strikes the hand where it will most hurt. "I went weakly down on my knees on the rug, and it wasn't all pretense," says Halley. Plainly his weakness is not due exclusively to pain, with which a steeplechase jockey always learns to live or to the shooting he has barely survived.

The humiliation is strong medicine as it turns out, however—as strong as Halley needs to begin to cure himself. This particular psychic violence is more than Charles Roland, Halley's father-in-law, had planned for him, yet Charles is the person who coerces Halley out of his misery by arranging a weekend in which Halley is subjected to numerous humiliations about his hand. He says it has been set up so that the villain Kraye will underestimate Halley when the ex-jockey begins to look into the attempted takeover of the Seabury racetrack. Yet by the end of the novel, Charles seems to have known that he could revivify the morose ex-champion by involving him in a case, especially one in which horse racing itself is threatened. Subjecting Halley to the insults of the Krayes and Mrs. Van Dysart (who has been invited solely because of her cruel tongue) may seem a brutality, yet it is like a painful operation that will restore the patient to health. Halley recognizes this process when Charles visits him in the hospital in the final chapter, telling Charles that he has been doing to Radnor what Charles had done for him on that terrible weekend at Charles's home: "Kicking him out of depression and into action" (651–52).

If Charles is the doctor of Halley's cure, then Zanna Martin is the nurse. During the investigation, Halley goes to the offices of a broker, Ellis Bolt. His intention is to pitch woo at Bolt's secretary and thereby get access to the files. The secretary is Zanna Martin, and his game becomes emotionally complicated when he gets to know her. Upon arriving at Bolt's offices, he does get a good look at her. He observes that she is "awkwardly placed" and that "perhaps she liked sitting in a potential draft and having to turn around every time someone came in" (531). She does not turn, however; she merely moves her head a fraction and points to a chair. As he waits, he looks over what he can see. She is in her late thirties, with a hairdo that is not right for her, and frumpy clothes. "It seemed as though she were making a deliberate attempt to be unattractive," observes Halley, "yet her profile . . . was pleasant enough" (532). After he talks with Bolt, he asks Martin if she will explain some things about investing. When she suggests he read a book, he asks her to dinner. She shudders and refuses, but Halley says, "If you will look at me, so that I can see all of your face . . . I will ask you again" (535). Finally he sees her entire face and insists again. She acquiesces with the words, "I'm not doing anything else tonight," and Halley explains:

Years of hopeless loneliness showed raw in the simple words. Not doing anything else, tonight or most nights. Yet her face wasn't horrific; not anything as bad as I had been prepared for. She had lost an eye and wore a false one. There had been some extensive burns and undoubtedly some severe fracture of the facial bones, but plastic surgery had repaired the damage to a great extent, and it had all been a long time ago. The scars were old. It was the inner wound which hadn't healed. Well . . . I knew a bit about that myself, on a smaller scale. (535)

Zanna Martin does not prove terribly important in working out the mystery, but she is important in moving along the parallel emotional plot: Halley's recovery from his injury. This secondary plot is interwoven with the mystery plot and adds much depth to Halley's character and enriches the book as a whole. On one level, it makes Halley more convincing as a human being. On another, it gives him an internal flaw that he must struggle to overcome as he battles external evil. Zanna is like an alter ego for Sid. As she is ashamed of her face, he is ashamed of his hand. As she has worked out careful strategies for avoiding exposure, he has worked out ways of getting by without taking the mutilated hand out of his pocket.

Yet what is one to do when fate has dealt such a hand? There is no going back. Halley cannot be a jockey again, and wallowing in self-pity has not helped. Zanna Martin will never be young and beautiful. When she was sixteen and a firework exploded against her cheek, it could have killed her. She says she sometimes wishes it had, something Halley obviously understands. The fact that "it wasn't anybody's fault" (538) is parallel to Halley's saying his racing accident was "one of those things" (543). At dinner, she asks why he never takes his hand from his pocket, and he, wishing he did not have to, shows it to her. She expresses pity, which leads to a small spat. Their scars are too raw. He says he can hide his hand. She says he cannot do the simplest things, like tying shoelaces or cutting steak. He is angry when reminded of his inabilities and upsets her. The irony is that her problem has been made small by her perception of Halley's problem, while he, for a moment, had forgotten his own when considering hers. They are beginning to help each other as they conclude dinner by deciding that pity is merely a form of tactless sympathy. It is bad manners that should not hurt either of them any more than other forms of bad manners. When Halley calls her a "liberator" at this point, he is predicting her role in helping him escape the psychological paralysis he has imposed upon himself (537–40).

Loosened by the brandy, she offers to turn her desk to face the clients if Halley will promise not to conceal his hand. He hesitates, but, "quaking at the thought of it," makes a pact with her. If she will rearrange her desk for a week, he will do as she asks. This is not an easy promise for either of them, but both are motivated by a desire to help each other. Halley remarks: "I had wanted to do something—anything—to help her. Anything. My God" (541). He does not seem to recognize that doing as she asks is not merely daring her into helping herself; it is helping him. Both of them are, through their pact, on their way to a different existence, one in which they can accept that they shall never have certain things or be able to do certain things that most other people take for granted. They are coming to an acceptance of their destinies by means of the healing power of human sympathy, another theme that recurs throughout Francis's novels. Reaching acceptance is not easy, however; years of hurt cannot be eliminated by a gallant promise. When Zanna finds out that Sid is not a shop owner as he had represented himself—that he was using her to get information about Ellis Bolt—she reacts as might be expected: "Why? Why did you play such a cruel game with me? Surely you could have gotten your information without that. Why did you make me change my desk round? I suppose you were laughing yourself sick all day Saturday thinking about it" (567–68). He tells her he upheld his part of their deal by exposing his hand at the Kempton races, but she, understandably, sends him home.

A writer with a more pessimistic attitude might have ended the relationship at this point, with Halley's interfering having done more harm than good, with Zanna tragically retreating even further into herself. One of Francis's most deep-seated beliefs, however, is in the tough resiliency of good people; they can take a physical or mental beating and spring back.[13] The next day Zanna sends Halley the information he wants with a note saying she is sorry. Halley calls it a "free pardon" (577) and goes to meet her after work. She is generous in understanding why Sid had to deceive her—perhaps a little too generous. She even thanks him for coming to see her. If this were not enough to induce enough guilt in Halley, the next appearance she makes in the plot is as the accidental holder of the case file that Bolt and the Krayes torture Halley to find. When they break his already useless hand again, he tells them Zanna has the file, and it becomes part of his touching the dark center of himself:

I thought about Bolt's going to Zanna Martin's front door. . . . I wondered for the hundredth time what he would do about that: whether he would harm her. Poor Miss Martin, whom life had already hurt too much. . . . I thought about the people who had borne the beatings and brutalities of the Nazis and of the Japanese and had often died without betraying their secrets. I thought about the atrocities still going on throughout the world, and the ease with which man could break man. (638)

This is a deliberate deception on Francis's part; clearly readers believe that Halley has tossed Zanna to the wolves. Actually, the villains have only broken his resolve to tell them nothing; Halley has, in a sense, gone into the heart of darkness and faced his own mortal limitations. This confrontation with his inability to resist—to protect Zanna and be the hero he would have wished to be—goes even deeper. It is the crisis that finally brings him to face the loss of the past. He knows himself better because he broke under torture; the most important part of his self-knowledge is the recognition of what he is now. He thinks about racing—about riding the Seabury course, about the weighing room, sitting on the scales—but he finally accepts his loss: "I thought: a fortnight ago I couldn't let go of the past. I was clinging to too many ruins, the ruins of my marriage and my racing career and my useless hand. They were gone for good now, all of them. There was nothing left to cling to" (639). He also thinks of the bomb that destroyed his apartment earlier in the novel. When he was told about it, he immediately thought about his past: "The letters from Jenny when she loved me. The only photograph of my mother and father. The trophies I won racing" (606). Facing death at the hands of the villains and remembering the bomb, he thinks, "Every tangible memory of my life had been blown away with a plastic bomb. I was rootless and homeless: and liberated" (639).

For the rest of the novel, after he escapes his would-be murderers, Halley is resolutely moving forward. He is not entirely free of the scars of having been without a father, of losing his career, hand, and wife, but he is trying to make a life with what he has. Parallel to Sid, Zanna has found a new liberation; she shows up at the hospital with a new hairdo, makeup, and smart clothes: "The scars were just as visible, the facial muscles as wasted as ever, but Miss Martin had come to terms with them at last" (656). She has a new, better-paying job in a bigger office. She thanks Sid for "changing everything" for her and adds, "I'll never forget how much I owe you" (656). There is a clear implication they will never meet again because she no longer needs him. Sid leaves his debt to her unstated. They have come together, and the healing power of the human bond has liberated them; yet ironically it causes them to drift apart, to end their relationship, because that is the goal of the healing.

A physical injury of the magnitude Halley suffered drags psychological problems in its wake, but Francis often provides another level of psychological damage in his hero, frequently related to the hero's childhood. Many of his heroes are orphans or emotionally estranged from their families. They are loners in the tradition of the hard-boiled hero. This estrangement also fulfills the function served by the physical limitations of a Francis hero, making him more human—more like ordinary mortals in his confrontation with evil. In *Nerve,* Rob Finn is estranged from his family because they are musicians and he disappointed them by becoming a jockey. He suffers further for being in love with his cousin, who will not reciprocate. In *Reflex,* Philip Nore is an orphan whose foster parents were a gay couple, and a large part of the plot consists of his seeking a lost sister. In *Banker,* Tim Ekaterin (besides trying to live down the suspicion that his family connection to the bank is unjustly helping him rise in his job) is in love with an ill coworker's wife, and his sense of honor prevents him from doing much about it. In *Proof,* Tony Beach is attempting to recover from the death of his wife, and in *Forfeit,* James Tyrone must deal with his wife's crippling poliomyelitis. Gene Hawkins of *Blood Sport* is rather unconvincingly suicidal and Matt Shore of *Rat Race* is so hurt by his broken marriage that he avoids becoming close to anyone else.

Halley, as the quintessential Francis hero, shares the orphan childhood and shattered marriage of other protagonists. He describes his blood parents in *Odds Against:* "My twenty-year-old father, working overtime for extra cash, had fallen from a high ladder and been killed three days before his wedding day, and . . . I had been born eight months later . . . My young mother, finding that she was dying of some obscure kidney ailment, had taken me from grammar school at fifteen, and because I was small for my age had apprenticed me to a racehorse trainer in Newmarket. . . . They had been good enough people, both of them" (473–74). Like his lively sidekick, Chico Barnes, Halley has learned to live with his parentless childhood, although there periodically surfaces the longing to have a traditional family. He, like several other Francis heroes, finds substitute fathers. The first is his trainer, who cared for him from age sixteen to twenty-one. Sid says bluntly, "I'd been lucky in my guvnor."[14]

There are a number of things Halley values from the "guvnor" besides learning to race. First, he learns about family life—how a man relates to his wife. Establishing relationships with other people is the only way to survive in a frequently hostile world; this is a recurring Francis theme. Second, by the example of his life-style and administrative ability, he teaches him how not to be overwhelmed or corrupted by money. This is another recurring motif. Francis's villains tend, despite their brutally relentless evil, to be corrupted rather than inherently evil. To remain uncorrupted is shown to be both difficult and the greatest test of manhood. Finally, the guvnor gives Halley the status of having come from his stables. This is akin to having received a good family name and substitutes for Sid's not having a heritage. At one point, a character attempts to insult Halley by saying the name "Sid" sounds like a plumber's assistant, but he merely says that plumbers' assistants are generally good people. The exchange plays on the idea that Sid

Halley has received nothing in his name and that a person's value is not determined by name alone.

Halley's most obvious substitute father in both *Whip Hand* and *Odds Against* is Admiral Charles Roland, ironically also his ex-father-in-law. Despite the enmity that has developed between Sid and Jenny, described by Halley as his "worst failure"(*WH,* 16; Francis never makes a marriage's dissolution trivial), Charles and Sid have become very close. In *Odds Against,* Charles is instrumental in helping Sid heal himself. In *Whip Hand* he draws Sid back into Jenny's life in a way not very different from the way he draws Sid into the Seabury racecourse case in *Odds Against.* Charles, as Sid says, is of a subtle mind. Charles also is a stiff-upper-lip Englishman, who holds the positive attributes of that stereotype while ultimately lacking the negative. At first, when Jenny announced to her father she was going to marry a jockey, Charles was extremely cold. He did not attend the wedding and spent months afterward in "frigid disapproval." Sid remarks: "I believed at the time that it was sheer snobbery, but it wasn't as simple as that. Certainly, he didn't think me good enough, but not only, or even mainly, on a class distinction level" (*OA,* 454). This wording is quite clear in acquitting Charles of class prejudice, although it seems perhaps Halley only wants to believe it had little to do with the initial reaction. Snobs are nearly always "bad blokes" in Francis. Later, when a rainy afternoon forces the two of them into a game of chess, Halley proves a formidable opponent and the traditional male respect for a worthy competitor draws them together. Charles is a man's man, courageous, honest, intelligent, caring, and loyal. As if that were not enough, he also grows to love racing. The bond that develops between them survives the ugliness of Sid and Jenny's divorce, and it is fairly obvious in *Whip Hand* that Sid takes on Jenny's case more out of friendship with her father than out of any residue of loyalty to her or the shame of her dragging the Halley name through the mud. It is also obvious from the beginning of *Odds Against* that Halley is willing to put up with much humiliation while trusting Charles's game to ensnare the Krayes.

The ugliness of Sid's divorce is explicit in *Whip Hand.* Jenny becomes a termagant who hates the sight of Sid and resents that he might be, even in her father's estimation, the man to help her out of the mess in which she finds herself. Sid would prefer not to stir up the memories of what had once been a good marriage. Charles may be playing his healing role once again, not intending to drive Sid and Jenny back together but simply to restore a more balanced view to their relationship.

He, after all, is Jenny's father and Sid's friend and would not like to be squeezed between them. The possibility that Jenny might be jailed for being duped by her boyfriend gives Charles the chance to bring Halley to her rescue. When Sid questions her about the con-man boyfriend, she explodes: " 'He was *fun*,' she said vehemently, unexpectedly. . . . She stopped. Her head swung my way with bitter eyes. 'He was full of life and jokes. He made me laugh. He was terrific. He lit things up. It was like . . . it was like . . .' She suddenly faltered and stopped, and I knew she was thinking, Like us when we first met. Jenny, I thought desperately, don't say it, please don't" (*WH,* 46). Halley then thinks: "How could people, I wondered for the ten thousandth useless time, how could people who had loved each other so dearly come to such a wilderness; and yet the change in us was irreversible, and neither of us would even search for a way back. It was impossible. The fire was out. Only a few live coals lurked in the ashes, searing unexpectedly at the incautious touch" (46–47).

The portrayal of this relationship is, I think, a bit too melodramatic, a little too pat, and Jenny's behavior toward Sid is so extraordinarily nasty it is hard to see that there could ever have been any reason to love her, and even less to help her. Perhaps one could accept her resentment of Sid's devotion to horse racing and its excitement: "Dedication and winning and glory," she says. "And me nowhere" (71), but when she throws his prosthesis charger on the bed and says, "It's disgusting. . . . It revolts me" (71), she seems cruel rather than merely surfacing her hurt. One of Francis's great abilities as a writer is that he can describe physical pain and terror in a cool, almost dispassionate way that makes the violence and fear into powerful experiences for the reader, but he slides a trifle toward hysteria in *Whip Hand* in creating his hero's psychological scar.

The psychological scar is not just the former marriage. The amputated hand plays once again a pivotal role. Having lost what was left of his mutilated hand in *Odds Against,* Halley has now nearly adjusted to having an electric hand that fits tightly on the stump of his arm. Francis makes the reader feel what this prosthesis is like and how it generates a routine for its owner, centered around recharging batteries. It is not, as in *Odds Against,* however, the lack of his hand that scars Halley so deeply in *Whip Hand.* It is cowardice. There are parallel investigations in *Whip Hand.* Sid is a full-time private investigator (Hunt Radnor Associates has gone from the scene) and needs to keep the business going. The novel begins with a brief chapter that is a paean to racing and then moves to a scene typical of the start of a hard-boiled mystery. The detective is relaxing (in this scene in his flat, recharging his prosthesis batteries), expecting nothing much, when a mysterious woman with trouble comes to the door. It is such a traditional beginning for hard-boiled novels that Woody Allen parodies it wonderfully in "Mr. Big"—private eye Kaiser Lupowitz is cleaning his thirty-eight when a buxom blonde comes in and asks him to find God, who is missing.[15] Francis avoids the most obvious clichés of these scenes by having Halley's visitor familiar to him, middle-aged, and not deceptive in what she asks.

Horses are not living up to their potential, and Halley must find out why. By chapter 7, however, he finds himself kidnapped, chloroformed, and dumped on a stable floor by thugs working for Trevor Deansgate, who has been described earlier as having a "faintly moist" hand (29), a frequently reliable indicator in Francis that the possessor is up to no good. Deansgate wants to stop Halley's inquiries but does not want to kill him. "Short of killing me," says Sid, "I didn't see how he could do it; and I was stupid" (107). Deansgate puts a shotgun against Halley's right wrist and cocks the firing mechanism. The threat of losing his only good hand is more than Halley can bear: "All the fear I'd ever felt in all my life was as nothing compared with the liquefying, mind-shattering disintegration of that appalling moment. It broke me in pieces. Swamped me. Brought me down to a morass of terror, to a whimper in the soul. And instinctively, hopelessly, I tried not to let it show" (108). Deansgate does not shoot off Halley's arm but orders him to Paris to wait until after the running of the Two Thousand Guineas. Halley meekly goes. Dumped at the airport, he goes unescorted and hides in a Paris hotel six days.

The rest of the book has Halley attempting to deal with his week of cowardice, another psychological scar for the hero. Francis has established his formula, but it is troubling here. The torture is gripping, of course, and Halley's being terrorized is plausible; the loss of his other hand is clearly worse than death to him. The extended period of his inaction, however, seems farfetched. Even when the gun is against his wrist, Halley has not reached bottom. Instinctively he tries not to let his terror show; he is not completely broken if his instinct still is there. Further, this is the same Halley, who, when tortured by the Krayes into a similar state of fear, sends Ellis Bolt to Chico Barnes's flat instead of Zanna Martin's.

Halley is reduced once again to a zombie-like state by the sense of worthlessness brought on by Deansgate's threat, and the rest of *Whip Hand* is parallel to *Odds Against* in that the restoration of Halley's sense of self-worth moves along with the working out of the mystery of how the horses are being disabled. Eventually Halley gets his revenge, but it is not clear he fully escapes the ramifications of his self-discovery under pressure. Deansgate has an opportunity to carry out his threat to mutilate Sid. This time, however, Sid seems more mentally defiant, though he is still shaken. He does not speak, and Deansgate goes into a virtual monologue of what has been going through his mind, interrupted only by Sid's remarks: "I said nothing"; "I didn't answer. Didn't move"; and "I thought numbly that I wasn't so sure, either, that I wouldn't rather be dead." But after begging God to give him courage, he finds anger: "He's making me sweat . . . wanting me to beg him . . . and I'm not . . . *not* . . . going to," he thinks, and "Sod you, I thought" (312–15). Francis creates a brilliant scene by avoiding a trite ending—the police rush in, for example, or Halley overcomes his enemy in a tussle. Deansgate simply leaves. Waiting in the garage to accomplish his revenge, he has come to see no point in it because, despite chasing Halley to Paris, he has come to believe that Sid is fearless. "I'd forgotten," says Deansgate, "what you're like. You've no bloody nerves." In both confrontations, Sid has appeared so stoic that the scene ends with the ironic line, " 'Isn't there *anything*,' [Deansgate] said bitterly, 'that you're afraid of?' " This may seem odd given the fact that Halley was frightened off, but Deansgate has evidently taken Sid's disappearance to have been a calculated ruse to make him feel safe. Sid was not really scared off because he did come back and take his revenge. Only Sid Halley (and the reader) know the extent of his fear. In the first confrontation, the reader experiences more of Halley's terror. In the second, the reader sees more of what Deansgate sees. Sid Halley is a man of extraordinary courage to everyone in the book, but readers have been let in on the secret. Courage is the external manifestation; it is not necessarily to the bone. The idea is existential in implication. As Jean-Paul Sartre said in many of his writings, other people's eyes are the mirrors in which one's identity is created.[16] What we do in the world, not what we think we do, is what is important. The man or woman who snivels when faced with terror (and Francis is quite clear it is impossible to know beforehand who will and who will not) becomes a coward. The man or woman who acts courageously, despite whatever is going on internally, is courageous. Deeds matter, not intentions. To paraphrase Chandler, a man of honor is a man of honor by instinct. Halley, a man of honor, is brave by instinct, which overrides his self-doubt, his dark night of the soul, when he faces the terror within him.

Daniel Roke

This existential problem is faced by other Francis heroes as well, though often it is only a situation in which the main character does not physically match people's preconceptions of his profession. Several jockeys (because they are steeplechasing, rather than flat, jockeys) surprise people because of their height. This is directly out of Francis's personal experiences. David Cleveland of *Slayride* is often told he appears too young to be the Jockey Commission's best investigator. In *For Kicks,* however, Daniel Roke grapples with the problem of appearance and identity perhaps more deeply than any other Francis hero.

Roke is an Australian whose parents were drowned in a sailing accident when he was eighteen. He assumed the parental role for his brother and sisters, sacrificing the pleasures of his early twenties so that they could have an education equal to that his parents had given him. He keeps telling himself he should be content with his situation, although he has had to give up the hope of becoming a barrister and even of racing when a leg he had broken at age twenty-two "caused the worst financial crisis of the whole nine years" and he "had no choice but to give up doing anything so risky."[17] It is easy to fit Roke into the Francis pattern. He is an orphan who has had to give up racing and who has an emotional uneasiness because he feels his life is dully slipping away from him. Not a detective, his chance to resolve the latter problem comes about when the earl of October, visiting Australia, asks him to investigate doping in England.

Roke must assume the guise of a dishonest stable hand. He carefully teaches himself to alter his Australian accent (mild because his parents were born in England) into a cockney. He wears pointed shoes and a leather jacket and startles the earl's butler when he assumes his full disguise. "Holy hell!" says the butler, ". . . You look shifty . . . and a bit . . . well . . . almost dangerous" (33). Roke soon finds that cab drivers demand to see his money before taking him anywhere and that stable hands ("the lads") live in acceptance of their secondary importance as human beings to their employers. Compared to the "almost aggressive egalitarianism of Australia," he finds this "extraor-

dinary, undignified, and shameful" (36). Yet he becomes vulnerable to
his assumed identity: his success and his survival depend upon assuming
his shifty role, and he has accepted the job because of uncertainty about
his actual identity. When the earl's sluttish daughter, Patty, leads him
into the barn, he kisses her and barely manages to resist her when she
peels off her dress. "I had an abrupt vision of myself as she must see
me, as I had seen myself in the long mirror in October's London house,
a dark, flashy-looking stableboy with an air of deceitfulness and an
acquaintance with dirt" (91). To have taken her offer would have been
immoral to Daniel Roke of Australia, but it would have been mere
pleasure to Danny Roke the shifty lad. Roke has the identity problem
faced by many actors, spies, and even businessmen who must feign
interest in extremely tedious clients. Who am I? he is asking himself.
What am I? If I act like a thug, is it because I am, at least in part,
a thug? He is angry at himself for yielding to Patty's kiss—for sliding
too far toward Danny Roke—and is aware that he has infuriated her
when Daniel Roke reasserts himself. Eventually the event is useful in
furthering the downward slide of Danny Roke but also indirectly nearly
brings about his death.

The problem intensifies when he relocates to Humber's stables. The
humiliations that Humber and his friend Adams heap upon their lads
must be endured if Roke is to find the solution to the mystery, yet
he is always struggling with the conflict between the pride inside him
and the sniveling exterior. He comments:

As the days of drudgery mounted up, I began to wonder if anyone who
embarked on so radical a masquerade really knew what he was doing.

Expression, speech, and movement had to be unremittingly schooled into
a convincing show of uncouth dullness. I worked in a slovenly fashion and
rode, with a pang, like a mutton-fisted clod; but as time passed, all these
deceptions became easier. If one pretended long enough to be a wreck, did
one finally become one? I wondered. And if one stripped oneself continuously
of all human dignity, would one in the end be unaware of its absence? I
hoped the question would remain academic and as long as I could have a
quiet laugh at myself now and then, I supposed I was safe enough. (121)

Roke is on a slippery slope, and when the sadistic Adams begins abusing
him, the crisis deepens. He takes the insults, the slaps, and other
indignities like a sniveling coward, and he begins to question what he
is. He catches himself in one of his notes impulsively begging the earl

of October to believe that he did not attack Patty as she, in revenge
for being spurned, has said. In disgust, he tears off "the pitiful words"
before he posts the letter (160).

Later he makes his biggest mistake in the presence of Patty's twin
sister, Elinor. She is not like Patty at all and is quite upset when she
hears from Patty that Roke has been unjustly accused. In her college
lodgings, he sees the life of study of which his parents' deaths has
robbed him. He turns away from the shelves, facing himself in a full-
length mirror. His hair is too long, his sideburns are flourishing, and
his skin has faded to yellow. He looks "disreputable and a menace to
society." Elinor remarks that he does not seem to like what he sees,
and he asks, "Would anyone?" She, however, implies that he is attractive.
She sees through the facade, at the very least to his handsomeness. "It
still happened," Roke thinks. "In spite of those terrible clothes, in spite
of the aura of shadiness, it could still happen. What accident . . .
decided that one should be born with bones of a certain design?" (172).
One's face and body, he goes on, are hereditary. One has no control
over appearance and should take no pride in it. He even expresses some
annoyance at having lost some business in Australia because men did
not like the way their wives looked at him. What seems to be happening
in this scene is that Elinor's incomplete glimpse of the man behind the
disguise helps Roke clutch on to the identity he has been nearly panicked
about losing. The meditation on heredity is quite Sartrean; it implies
that a man is what he makes of himself (his essence) rather than what
he is born into (his being). As if to reassert who he is under the
disguise, Roke cannot help but make a seemingly harmless remark to
Elinor, but one that his assumed character is unlikely to know—that
the source of a quotation is Marcus Aurelius. He nearly tells her the
truth about himself, but he makes up something about his schooling.
The quotation plainly relates to the situation he has gotten himself into:
"Nowhere either with more quiet or more freedom from trouble does
a man retire than into his own soul." He also tells her that it is from
the "section about learning to be content with your lot. I suppose I
remember it because it is good advice and I've seldom been able to
follow it" (175–76). This brief reassertion of his real identity is something
he has dearly needed, though it leads to his nearly being killed.

There are later moments in *For Kicks* in which the problem of his
identity recurs, but he is defiantly Daniel Roke of Australia when he
confronts the evildoers. Adams orders him to remove his helmet in the
presence of a lady, Elinor, and he does not. Adams asks whether Roke

might be the kind of man who would need to tranquilize himself to face a violent horse (as Roke has earlier claimed), and Elinor says, "Of course not." Humber, who does not understand, remarks that Roke seems different, and Adams, reflecting Roke's own quandary, says, "Roke, damn him to hell, is God knows what." Roke is relieved not to have to cringe before Adams and Humber before they try to kill him (212). Afterward Roke's appearance plagues him as the police arrest him for murder. A doctor who comes to help Elinor at Roke's behest remarks that Daniel did not seem like the usual "tearaway," but when the police come, the stereotype is reestablished. Roke momentarily tries to convince the doctor of his innocence, without knowing why it seems important to do so, though it is obviously part of his asserting his self. The doctor ignores him. When the police shove Roke past the college women, Roke is humiliated at their seeing him as a prisoner, and says he could have stood it better if they were men, implying that his feigned cowardice and criminality have damaged his manhood. The police, however, remark upon how Roke seemed totally unaffected by being marched past the girls.

The hell of other people's eyes continues as he takes several days to convince the police of his innocence. When they look at him, they ask, "How can we believe a yob like you?" and Roke thinks: "Yob. One of the leather boys. Tearaway. Rocker. I knew all the words. I knew what I looked like. What a millstone of a handicap" (237). When the earl of October reappears, Roke, unable to change clothes before leaving jail, is confronted by a suspicious waiter on the train who demands to see his first-class ticket. When he does change back into his own clothes, he contemplates himself in a mirror: "There was the man who had come from Australia four months ago . . .; there was his shell, anyway. Inside I wasn't the same man, nor ever would be again" (243). It is worth noting also that when he sees Patty and Elinor after cleaning up that Patty does not recognize him, whereas Elinor says hesitantly, "You don't look the same . . . but you're Daniel" (244), showing that she may be the only character who can see below the surface. At the conclusion of the novel, Roke is certain enough of what he wishes to be that he "irrationally" sets aside his life as a horse breeder in order to take up intelligence work. The trial by fire he has gone through has made him understand himself more clearly. Coming so close to losing his identity has made him grasp it all the better.

Conclusion

In this chapter, I have concentrated on the four novels that exemplify Francis's approach to characterizing his hero and are among the best representatives of this approach, within the confines of his formula and genre. When a writer creates as many novels and heroes as Francis has, he will obviously invite relative comparisons. *Whip Hand* is not quite as convincing as *Odds Against,* but that does not imply it is a bad book. *Whip Hand* occupies a high place among the Francis novels. It is psychologically probing compared to most of the trivial books that burden the shelves of hard-boiled novels. Yet in the body of Francis's work, there are no outstanding failures. There is enough variation of locale, character, and plot that he does not seem repetitive, and yet he works with discipline within an amiable formula. Much of what makes Francis one of the best in his genre is his deliberate attempt to complicate the main character. Like Chandler's heroes, Francis's are the modern equivalent of knights in an unchivalric world, and they frequently (as in Sir Walter Scott's *Ivanhoe*) are forced into a decisive battle weakened by wounds. As is appropriate for the twentieth century, however, Francis recognizes the profound weaknesses induced by psychological trauma and the difficulty of overcoming it. It is an essential part of his formula, and he is at his best when the complexity of the psychological scars of his hero approach the complexity of Sid Halley's. When the hero is not a superman, he is all the more credible.

Halley is self-absorbed with his courage, his honor, his body, and racing. He has a limited ability to express his emotion. "It would go against the grain to show it," said Francis of him.[18] Toward the end of *Whip Hand* after he has rescued Jenny, her remarks point up these imperfections: "You're so hard. Hard on yourself. Ruthless to yourself. I couldn't live with it. No one could live with it. Girls want men who'll come to them for comfort. Who say, I need you . . . But you . . . you can't do that. . . . I need a husband who's not so rigidly in control of himself. I want someone who's not afraid of emotion, someone uninhibited, someone weaker. I can't live in the sort of purgatory you make of life for yourself. I want someone who can break down. I want . . . an ordinary man" (285). Sid is neither ordinary nor a saint; in Chandler's words, he is plainly "the best man in his world and a good enough man for any world." This is true of all of Francis's protagonists. The whodunit aspect of Francis's novels may hook readers and drag them along, but it is his embellishments of character that make the best books stand out. This is exactly what the jockey-turned-author intends. Saying that Francis's strength is in the plot is like saying that *Citizen Kane* is about a guy who loses a sled.

All the novels are not equally as elaborate in embellishing character. *Dead Cert* is an excellent thriller, though it lacks the psychological dimension Francis uses so effectively in *Nerve* and then the Halley books. Sometimes, as in *Break In* and *The Danger,* the psychological dimension of the hero is present but thin. At least once, it is extremely unconvincing—in *Blood Sport*—probably because the first-person narrative style does not lend itself well to the cool analysis of the hero's suicidal tendencies. Nonetheless, these are relative comparisons, and the Francis formula always inserts enough interesting ingredients to overcome any individual slips.

One final mental scar that is always convincing in Francis is one that must be personal to the author—the loss of racing. Like Halley, many of his other characters must face the fact that they will never ride in a competitive race again. Men age quickly, and with the loss of youth comes the loss of the ability to be effective athletes, especially in a bone-breaking sport. *Whip Hand's* prologue of Halley's recurring dream serves to deepen his character and make us aware of the lost hand; it also serves to remind us of Dick Francis himself, an author who would likely toss all of his celebrated books aside if he could be carried once more over the enormous hedges at the Grand National, to feel the heat and mud and wind of a furious steeplechase.

Chapter Three
Fathers and Sons
The Missing Father

In bending the hard-boiled tradition to create his own distinctive product, Francis wraps his novels around the thematic question of manhood. This is not "manhood" in the sense of "mankind," although most of his larger assumptions—you are what you do; you must accept your limitations, face them, and go on—he would philosophically apply equally to men and women. The Zanna Martin–Sid Halley parallel is a perfect example of the more universal application of his ethics. On the other hand, Francis does not presume to deal with his women characters in the same way he deals with his men, having once said that he could not create a woman protagonist because he cannot place himself in a woman's mind.[1]

The questions "What is a man?" "How should he act?" and "What is his essence?" are all answered by implication in any representation of a character who is a hero. A strong moral sense is important in the hard-boiled tradition, and for Francis it is a primary element. A code of values is shown in action in a mode not much different from the didactic legends of medieval literature that fostered the codes of nobility. The deeds of Roland, Siegfried, and Parsifal teach by example what any knight (noble man) should do. How Alan York and other Francis heroes behave is also intended to tell us how a man should live. The transmission of male values between father and son should therefore be of crucial significance, and it is, but not as might be expected.

In the hard-boiled tradition, examples of novels that pay much attention to the hero's familial relationships are rare. Like the traditional American western hero, the hard-boiled detective is usually a loner with profound loyalties but few of the complications of wife, children, and parents. Ex-wives are less rare, but mostly these men get what family they have from their friendships. Francis's heroes typically are lone wolves. Sid Halley, Matt Shore of *Rat Race,* and Jonah Dereham of *Knockdown* are divorced. Tony Beach of *Proof* and Kelly Hughes of

Enquiry are widowers. Rob Finn of *Nerve* and Tim Ekaterin of *Banker* are in love with women they cannot have. James Tyrone of *Forfeit* is married, but because of the paralysis of his wife, their marriage consists mostly of his duty to her. Jonathan Derry of *Twice Shy* has a marriage strained by their inability to have a child. There is also Edward Link of *Smokescreen,* who is happily married—a family man's family man— but his immediate family is peripheral to the story and seems too much of a device whose purpose is mainly to show that the home life of a movie star is usually not as glamorous as the public assumes, reflecting Francis's warning to would-be jockeys that the glamor of any profession does not last very long (*SQ,* 51, 109). After the first chapters, most of *Smokescreen* has Link in South Africa, connected to his family only by telephone, so in effect he too becomes a lone wolf. Interestingly enough also, Link, the remarkably stable and (for a Francis hero) untroubled narrator, remembers his father yelling himself hoarse as he taught the boy to ride (23). Edward, however, recalls this with a smile, and there is no sign that this memory is typical or that he will treat his own children harshly. The father plays no other role in the book, though Edward was motherless in his teens, a variation on Francis heroes' recurring fatherlessness that lacks the intensity of the usual pattern. It perhaps is one reason Link is one of Francis's least interesting main characters.

The isolation of the hero becomes even more pronounced when the parental relationships are examined. Orphans are so frequent in Francis novels that there is a great temptation to turn these occurrences back upon the author and make Oedipal hay of them. After all, it is easy to turn the recurring motif of a jockey facing retirement back upon the real problem faced by the author when he quit racing. Francis admits that much of himself is revealed in his heroes, such as the painful shoulder separation that both he and Jonah Dereham of *Knock-down* suffer (*SQ,* 192). Edward Link's memory of learning to ride is nearly identical to Francis's memory of learning to ride in *The Sport of Queens* (20). So why not infer something about Francis's own relationship with his father? In his autobiography both his grandfather and father are described as stern. Yet when directly asked, he has been adept at avoiding comment on the subject. Diana Cooper-Clark asked whether Francis was drawn to fathers and sons for any particular reason. Francis's answer was: "No, I'm not drawn to father figures. In fact I don't really like father figures but I do like elderly men who are modern in the way that they think . . . I like elderly men to move with the

times and if they do . . . they are very fine, good people to talk to."[2]
Francis was more direct in answering John C. Carr, perhaps because
the question was more direct. Carr tries to make Francis draw a
comparison to the father and son in *Bonecrack* and his father and
himself. Francis does not take the bait, so Carr asks bluntly if George
Vincent Francis was stern. Francis answers: "Yes, he was stern. But he
didn't knock you about or anything, although he did give me a good
hiding once [*laughs*] and I never forgot it. But he wasn't one for giving
credit unless it was—that is, at the time. People used to come up to
me and say, 'Oh, well done, Dick, you did great things,' and Father
would say, 'Oh, you've got another one to do tomorrow.' "[3] In *Bonecrack*,
Neil Griffon's father is also described as not believing in beating but
punishes psychologically quite harshly. It is an interesting parallel, though
it must be remembered that a writer often distorts a real situation in
order to make it less ambiguous for fiction, and the elder Griffon is
more likely to be an exaggeration of George Vincent or a literal
representation of someone anonymous. There is nothing Francis has
written that would indicate his father was as insensitive as the elder
Griffon.

What is ultimately important is not whether or how Francis got
along with his father but what manifests itself in his writings. It is,
after all, an author's works and what can be shown to be vibrating in
the text that matter, not what skeletons may be imagined rattling in
his house and head. The facts are that Philip Nore of *Reflex,* Sid
Halley, Daniel Roke, Roland Britten of *Risk,* Kit Fielding of *Break In*
and *Bolt,* and Jonah Dereham of *Knockdown* are orphaned. Generally
the loss of parents is sudden: falling off a ladder, heart attack, auto
accident, a sailing accident, a riding accident, a cerebral hemorrhage.
Sometimes there is mention of the father's (and mother's) inadequacy
before death. Tim Ekaterin's parents were hard-core gamblers and
alcoholic spendthrifts. Tim describes his father as "a weak, friendly,
unintelligent man. Not bad as a father. Not much good at anything
else."[4] Britten's father died in "a pointless sort of accident," and his
mother, "a rotten businesswoman," killed herself with two hundred
aspirins, leaving a note which said only, "Dear Ro, Sorry, Love, Mum."[5]
Charles Todd of *In the Frame* describes his father, who died when
Charles was twenty-two, as "middle-aged, middle of the road, expert
at his chosen job, but unlikely to set the world on fire."[6] The dead
parents, and particularly the father, tend to be weak or hopelessly
mediocre and do not exercise much control over the son. At the same

time, the hero almost always remarks something in their favor—they were good-hearted or something similar that seems like wishfulness. Daniel Roke is a rarity when we discover that his father was a "good" barrister (*FK*, 13).

Parents who manage to survive to the beginning of a Francis novel are not warmly portrayed. The estrangement is usually accepted by the hero as being a difference of temperament decreed by fate, but there is usually a disturbing coldness about the parents' behavior. Rob Finn has none of the musical inclinations or talent that are so prominent in his family, and he is treated with condescension because of having chosen racing as a profession. Rob's father has the personality of a cipher and always treats him "with polite friendliness," but he is "not really interested"[7] His mother gives him the same greeting she gives everyone from "impresarios to back-row chorus singers and when applied to me," says Rob, "still utterly lacked any maternal quality. She was not a motherly person in any way . . . I never expected a broad motherly bosom to comfort my childish woes, nor a sock-darning, cakemaking mum to come home to" (23–24). It is easy to read his desperate love for his first cousin Joanna as a psychological desire to become once again part of his family.

Flying Finish gives us a character who actively dislikes his family. Because he will be the earl of Creggan when his father dies, Henry Grey is constantly having eligible, wealthy girls pushed at him to restore the declining aristocratic fortunes. When the earl dies, Henry thinks, "I tried to grieve for him, and had recognized that my only strong emotion was an aversion to being called by his name."[8] His mother, insensitive to Henry's feelings, cries "hysterical tears" because he refuses to assume his aristocratic role, and his sisters bitterly attack him (120). Henry in many ways is like an adolescent attempting to contrast himself with his family in order to establish his own identity.

The relationship between Alan York and his father in *Dead Cert* is about the closest in all the Francis novels. When Alan's horse is tripped in exactly the way that killed his friend Bill, he is pummeled by the horses following him and then kicked unconscious by one of the malefactors. He regains consciousness in a hospital with a concussion and a temporarily damaged memory. The doctor urges him to sleep, and when he awakens he says, "I fell out of a tree." He has remembered an incident in his boyhood: "I hit my head, and when I woke my father was kneeling beside me." When he rolls his head to the side, his father is sitting by his bed, "sunburnt, fit, distinguished, and at forty-six looking still a young man" (162). The elder York casually says that he flew up when he was told Alan was in the hospital and he thought he had "better take a look." When Alan reacts to the pain of his broken ribs, his father grows anxious and asks Alan to promise not to ride in an important race in about a week. Comments Alan: "When I saw the anxiety in his face I understood for the first time in my life how much I meant to him. I was his only child, and for ten years, after my mother died, he had reared me himself, not delegating the job . . . as many a rich man would have done, but spending time playing with me and teaching me, and making sure I learned in my teens how to live happily and usefully under the burden of extreme wealth" (163–64). Recognizing that he owes his father so much, Alan takes the extraordinary step (for a Francis hero) of passing up the big race.

In the next chapter, Mr. York is gruff in handling his cranky son, ordering him to drink a stiff brandy at ten-thirty in the morning. Alan resists. "Drink it and shut up," Mr. York says, and Alan furiously swallows it. This episode reveals a father caring for his son, pushing him when necessary, and later when Alan's grumpiness has been somewhat suppressed by the liquor, Mr. York teases him—by calling him "Sherlock Holmes reincarnated"—into explaining the mystery to Inspector Lodge. "Don't be infuriating, Alan," says York. "Elucidate" (176). These two scenes of interaction between father and son reveal nothing spectacular in father-son relationships. They plainly love one another. The father admires and respects the son but knows when his boy needs a stern prod. The son admires and respects the father and appreciates the sacrifices made on his behalf. But in the more than twenty novels that follow *Dead Cert,* this relationship is unique. There may be love in other cases—in those unusual instances where the son knows his father—but there is usually a coarse edge to it. The father or both parents are inept or insensitive, and the son's love has an unhappy desperation in it.

The Griffons and the Riveras

Bonecrack provides one of the most interesting opportunities to explore Francis's fathers and sons by featuring parallel pairs in the hero's father and the villain. Because *Bonecrack* shows the most complete and complex working out of the father-son themes, the development of these relationships must necessarily be traced in close detail to get at the ambiguities and moral truths that Francis unfolds.[9] The novel opens with the abduction of Neil Griffon. Because he has temporarily taken over his father's stables, Neil has been mistaken for the elder Griffon, who is laid up with a broken leg from an auto accident. He does not, however, let the threatening boss of his kidnappers know that he has intended to stay on for only the minimum time it would take to find a replacement for his father. Withholding this fact seems to save his life; the boss tells Neil that he wants him to hire his son to be a jockey. Despite the Griffons' already having England's second-best jockey on payroll, they are being coerced to place an inexperienced rider on the best horses, merely because the spoiled boy wants to ride them. If Neil does not cooperate, the stables will be destroyed.

Neil seems largely to have returned home in order to reestablish a family relationship with his father. While describing Mr. Griffon's coldly efficient secretary, Margaret, he remarks: "She demanded no human response, and he [Mr. Griffon] was a man who found most human relationships boring. Nothing tired him quicker than people who constantly demanded attention for their emotions and problems, and even social openers about the weather irritated him."[10] Neil says that after the threat, he could no longer turn the stable over to a replacement because it would be like giving someone a grenade with the pin removed, and he lies to his employer about the seriousness of his father's condition in order to remain at the stable. Yet the impression given is that Neil is sticking around, not unwillingly, to seek a rapprochement with his father, to grasp some of the love with which the stony old man has never been generous. Here is, despite its unpleasantness, a situation in which Neil can both do something his father respects—train horses— and protect him.

When Alessandro Rivera, the jockey, shows up, the resemblance between he and his father, Enso, ends "with the autocratic beak of the nose," "the steadfast stoniness of the black eyes," and the "definite, unaccented, and careful" voice (36–37). There are many obvious contrasts. Enso is fat; Alessandro is "emaciated." The boy is arrogant but apparently to cover insecurity. He is obviously spoiled, saying that he will neither feed the horses nor clean their boxes; he does not even wish to be an apprentice. He shows his first bit of character when faced with the papers that will make him an apprentice. Neil expects him not to return, but he does, with his father's signature on the papers. Neil observes, "What I thought was that the son was not as criminal as his father. The son had taken the legal obligations of the

apprenticeship form seriously. But his father had not" (43). This
difference between Alessandro and his brutal father will ultimately result
in the boy's maturing into manhood.

Immediately after, Neil goes to the hospital, and the reader is given
a fuller look at the sad relationship between the Griffons. Neil describes
the dismal private room and tells how the doctor urged him to put
his father in a public ward so that the other people would keep his
mind occupied. Neil, however, understanding his father, did not. When
he first comes in, the old man is asleep. He looks "defenseless in a
way he never did when he was awake"; "he no longer seemed to be
disapproving of nineteen-twentieths of what occurred. A lock of gray-
white hair curved softly down over his forehead, giving him a friendly
gentle look which was hopelessly misleading" (44). This fatherly appearance is immediately shattered by the reality of Neil's memories:
"The severity with which he had used me had not, after all, been
rejection and dislike, but lack of imagination and an inability to love.
He had not believed in beating, but he had lavishly handed out other
punishments of deprivation and solitude, without realizing that what
would have been trifling to him was torment to me" (44). Neil, then,
is an abused child—and the scars of his humiliation and shame are as
deep as if they had been physical. When he ran away from Eton, his
father never forgave him, and his aunt relayed the comment that Mr.
Griffon had provided him with horses to ride and taught him obedience,
"and what more could any father do for his son?" (44). Griffon did
not even try to get his son back, and it is finally Neil who, after many
years, approaches his father at Ascot and meets with him regularly
though with no real warmth. After more than a dozen years, the
memories of being locked in his bedroom for three or four days at a
time are still so disturbing that Neil cannot sleep in his old bedroom
with the door closed.

The old man is adamantly opposed to Neil's running the stables.
He says Neil does not know a damn thing about it and contemptuously
says, "I can't see you supplying winners." When Neil says he does
not see why not, the old man cruelly asks, "Can't you? . . . Can't
you, indeed?" Neil's answer is an offer to start over: "Not if you will
give me your advice" (47). The gesture throws the old man; he comes
up with no answer but repeats his order to get someone else. Later
visits repeat the pattern of this one. When Neil tells him about the
new apprentice, lying to cover up how Enso has forced the boy on
them, Griffon eventually acquiesces. When he tells the old man how

the horses are working, however, his father says he wants a list of the horses' progress from Etty Craig, Neil's assistant and the head lad. Griffon looks for resentment, but Neil does not show it, commenting, "The antagonism of an aging and infirm father toward a fully grown and healthy son was a fairly universal manifestation throughout nature, and I wasn't fussed that he was showing it. But all the same I was not going to give him the satisfaction of feeling he had scored over me" (67). He even offers to schedule the race entries with Etty when his father admits he has been too busy with X-rays and treatments, but old Griffon petulantly says no; he will do them. Neil offers to bring him some champagne, which his father believes has healing properties, and the old man only nods. "The day my father thanked me would be the day his personality disintegrated" (67), says Neil.

Old Griffon is no hard-cased curmudgeon with a soft interior; he is flint all through. Neil's persistence can be interpreted as another instance of a Francis hero reaching out to save misguided or psychically wounded persons from themselves. Also recognizable is the pattern of the hero doing the best he can with what fate has given. It rings chillingly true as a representation of the dependence that arises between an abuser and the abused. The old man is the only father Neil has known, and as horrible as that childhood was, there is no way to replace it. He seeks desperately to redeem it—by gaining his father's approval, by being strong against Rivera when the old man cannot be strong. Although this blighted relationship does not appear to have affected his excellent relationship with his girlfriend, Gillie, Neil's hesitation to commit himself to matrimony is revealed with the lame excuse he would make a "lousy husband" (95); it is easy to read a fear of love into it.

Neil soon assumes a fatherly role with Alessandro. The boy shows up in a chauffeur-driven white Mercedes, wearing "superbly cut jodhpurs and glossy brown boots," and looking "more like an advertisement in *Country Life* than a working rider" (54). The struggle of wills has already begun and is more firmly established by Alessandro's demanding to know where Neil has been and Neil shooting back, "Where have you?" Only a few minutes later, Neil resists the temptation of humiliating the boy by putting him on a difficult mount. He passes this decision off as not wanting to risk an injury to a good horse. Subsequent events imply, however, that he does not wish to hurt the pompous, spoiled boy; instead he wants to free Alessandro of the misleading influence of his monstrous father. When Neil puts him under the command of Etty Craig, Alessandro says, "I do not take orders from a woman" (55), the typical response of an adolescent who has not yet established a secure identity. Neil appears to be deliberately humiliating Alessandro just to get rid of him, but, ultimately this too, if degrading, is degradation similar to that done to Sid Halley by Charles Roland. It results in Alessandro's beginning to understand what it is to be a man. Neil even tells Etty later that they will "hope to teach him better ways" (61).

He does not learn easily. When Etty calls him "Alex" and orders him to hold a horse, he reacts "like a throttled volcano" and once again says he will not take orders from a woman (58). "My father will not let you treat me like this," he says. Neil appeals to his pride: "Your father . . . must be overjoyed to have a son who needs to shelter behind his skirts. . . . Your father said I was to give you good horses to ride in races. Nothing was mentioned about bowing down to a spoiled little tin god. . . . Tell him what you like. But the more you run to him, the less I'll think of you" (59). Alessandro retorts that he does not care what Neil thinks, but Neil flatly says, "You're a liar." To be a man, you must not only pay your dues but be accepted by other men as their equal. It is important what Neil thinks. Why, after all, does this boy want to race on good horses? In order to achieve recognition. What he has not learned from his father is that he cannot get into the fraternity without taking the hazing. Note how Neil, in the image of Alessandro's hiding behind Enso's skirts, has compared the boy's father to a woman.

The relationship continues rockily for a few days; then Alessandro squeals to his father. Alessandro even says "matter-of-factly" that Enso will kill Neil and, reports the hero, "The thought of it did not surprise or appall him" (64). He underestimates his mentor, however, who is uncowed by the threat, and admits that Neil confuses him (64). Alessandro is going through the frightening process of change. He is discovering his father cannot get him everything he wants, an ironic opposite to Neil's father, who has always given little. After Etty deliberately puts Alessandro on a rambunctious mount that exposes the boy's inexperience, Alessandro becomes more human as he and Neil soothe the horse. Neil explains the folklore of the "Boy's Grave," (the color of the flowers on this anonymous suicide's grave are supposed to predict the Derby winner) and reminds us how the father-son relationships are counterpoint. "It was a pity . . . that he [Alessandro] was as he was. With a different father, he might have been a different person. But with a different father, so would I. And who wouldn't" (74). The last line seems to dismiss the thought, but in fact it defines the problem.

Neil is also facing the question of identity. He is asking himself, "Who am I?"—in a large way, the theme of the book. You can take the boy away from his father, but can you take the father out of the boy? Alessandro needs freedom to become a man. Neil has had nothing but freedom.

Alessandro shows some backbone when he insists on riding the horse that humiliated him. Later Neil understands and marvels at what he has failed thus far to recognize: "This [urge to ride] was no idle fancy. It was revealing itself all too clearly as a consuming ambition: an ambition strong enough to make him starve himself, take orders from a woman, and perform what were evidently miracles of self-discipline, considering that it was probably the first time in his life that he had had to use any" (103). Although he is rude when he regains consciousness after being bucked to the ground by the fractious horse, he tells his chauffeur that Neil would not hurt him (81). Nonetheless, Enso cruelly breaks a second horse's leg as he has done before, in order to make Neil obey him. The interesting result, however, is that when Neil confronts Alessandro with the proof, the boy seems genuinely upset. The parallels converge again as Neil thinks:

He went away and left me speechless.
He couldn't talk to his father.
Enso would give Alessandro anything he wanted, would smash a path at considerable trouble to himself, and would persist as long as Alessandro hungered, but they couldn't talk.
And I . . . I could lie and scheme and walk a tightrope to save my father's stables for him.
But talk with him, no, I couldn't. (89)

The relationship between Neil and his father thaws somewhat on his next hospital visit. The old man complains that Neil has not tried hard enough to find a replacement, that Neil has entered the horse Pease Pudding in the wrong race, and that he has brought the wrong vintage of champagne. Neil fights back, and Griffon is stunned. Neil thinks, "I . . . knew that things would never be quite as they had between us. Thirty-four, I thought ruefully; I had to be thirty-four before I entered this particular arena on equal terms" (97). Neil refuses again to replace himself, and his father changes the subject. As Neil is about to leave, the old man makes a gruff gesture of his own; he offers Neil some champagne. "Not as symbolic a gesture as a pipe of peace,"

comments Neil, "but just as much of an acknowledgement, in its way"
(99).

Coming off this apparent tightening of his relationship with his father,
Neil trusts Alessandro to exercise the most valuable horse of the stable,
Archangel. He rides it well, as even Etty grudgingly admits. Neil then
puts Alessandro on another horse and asks him to appraise its performance. Not only does Alessandro restrain himself from overpushing the
horse, but for the first time he makes an objective self-assessment. This
foreshadows his surprising evaluation of how to ride Pulitzer later in
the novel (123). But his old traits are still there when Neil chooses
another jockey to ride Archangel in a race; Alessandro gives the jockey
a look that "was pure Rivera. Actively dangerous: inured to murder"
(106). But after a firm talking to, Alessandro, though still angry, seems
to realize that professional riding, which he started on a whim, has
now become more (107). This reveals another Francis theme: the
discovery of the underlying world of racing, where vanity and greed
are less important than the process itself.

Although Alessandro still tells Neil to do what Enso says, when they
have a confrontation about which horse Alessandro will ride, there is
a definite change in the boy. He now says, "My father says I am to
tell you that you must," and "He says I must insist" (112). There is
a slight but important distancing occurring, a distancing that will mature
the brat. Alessandro even gets angry at his father for ordering another
attack on a horse. As Neil drives Alessandro to the races, they have a
long conversation about the struggle. Neil tells the boy to stop relying
on his father. "It is natural to rely on one's father," is the response.
Neil counters with, "I ran away from mine when I was sixteen."
"Obviously he did not, like mine, give you everything you wanted."
"No. . . . I wanted freedom" (121–22). This is the first of several
car trips together, and in each one Neil enlarges his fatherly role,
advising Alessandro not just on riding but on behavior, such as bragging
and despairing about mistakes. Alessandro loosens up and discusses the
last time he saw his mother, when he was six.

The tug of war between Neil and his father resumes—"the champagne
truce had barely seen me out the door," says Neil (125)—as the old
man telephones the press and tells them his horse Pease Pudding does
not stand a chance. Neil's instructing the jockey to ignore his father's
instructions does not help their relationship, even when the horse wins.
Old Griffon is furious about having his authority compromised and
refuses champagne because it might seem like a celebration. The race

helps Alessandro, however. He admits, though humility is hardly easy to him, that he could not have ridden as well as Neil's choice. When Alessandro loses later, he accepts the result without fury (140), and when outridden by the Champion Jockey, he says he will improve. He proves to have ability in racing tactics and gets noticed for winning. He even controls his "habitual arrogance" (141).

Enso returns, however, demanding that Alessandro ride Archangel, an impossibility. Neil cannot risk a great and expensive horse's life on an amateur rider, but he says nothing, which the madman takes for acceptance. Alessandro later begs Neil to put him on Archangel, but he seems as worried about what his father will do as he does about his fantasy. The boy actually tells his father that it is not right for him to ride Archangel (161). Later Alessandro says to Neil in exasperation, "You and my father, you tear me apart." Neil responds, "You'll have to choose your own life" (147). A brutal climax, however, is on the way, and it has less to do with Archangel than with the fatherly role Neil has assumed. Alessandro is "going to kick the problem of too much father" (148), but Enso, whose obsessive love for his son has nearly ruined the boy, will not let him go. "Alessandro was halfway across the bridge," thinks Neil. "And Enso guessed it. Enso was not going to allow me to take his son" (149).

The final step in Alessandro's movement toward adulthood is the death of Enso, which takes place, symbolically enough, at the crossroads of the Boy's Grave. The full irony of Alessandro's "epitaph" for his father is obvious. "He gave me everything," he says. Yet Enso did not give his son the most precious gift, the freedom to be a man. What started for Alessandro as another present from his father has turned into a lesson about achievement: the process of getting is as important as the reward. Everyone at the end of the novel seems to assume that Neil will have Alessandro banished from racing, but when the boy, with strain having aged him and "little in the black eyes except no hope at all," reappears at the stables to ask for his winnings, Neil tells him that he has kept Alessandro from punishment. The Jockey Club has settled all blame on the dead Enso, and Neil says he sees no reason to revenge himself on Alessandro. The boy then confesses he asked his father to force Neil to back down, but Neil replies, "Just how many fathers would do as he did? How many fathers, if their sons said they wanted to ride Archangel in the Derby, would go as far as murder to achieve it?" (186). A father who will not refuse for his son's own good is a madman. Alessandro accepts this with "no comfort." Neil thinks:

"He didn't look the same boy as the one who had come from Switzerland three months before, and in fact he wasn't. All his values had been turned upside down, and the world as he had known it had come to an end. To defeat the father, I had changed the son. Changed him at first only as a solution to a problem, but later also because the emerging product was worth it. It seemed a waste, somehow, to let him go." Alessandro will become Neil's second-best jockey, and the boy runs down the drive, "leaping into the air as if he were six" (187).

A happy ending? Not exactly. This scene is darkened by the parallel struggle. The novel ends as happily as possible, but Francis does not allow the total comfort of the lie that all things work out for the better. As the novel developed, it seemed to be moving inexorably toward a solution for both sons. Alessandro's problem with a bad father is resolved; the only solution to Neil's problem, however, is to stop letting the relationship bother him. The champagne truce seemed to imply that the coldness was abating. Yet the last time old Griffon is shown, the old man looks "even more forbidding than usual" because of the gunplay with the Rivera gang. Archangel has won the Derby under Neil's care, but Griffon wants only to complain about the handling of Enso. Neil answers "neutrally" and "patiently," but the sad picture is of a man waiting like a helpless boy for his father to show approval, affection, recognition. Griffon even implies that Neil's broken collarbone is "chicken feed." The reader, however, who has gone through the excruciating breaking of that bone by Enso's thugs, will plainly feel the abhorrent callousness. Neil asks when he will be out of the hospital, and Griffon says maliciously "Sooner than you'd like, perhaps." Neil protests, "I couldn't wish you to stay here," but the wording implies he is resisting the impulse. When Neil says, "The sooner the better," for the old man's getting out, he tries to mean it. Griffon then makes a big point of telling Neil to tell Etty what a good job she did with Archangel—not a decent word for his own son but praise for his head lad (180). Neil finally resolves the problem with his father, but not happily: " 'He gave me everything,' Alessandro had said of his father. I would have said of mine that he gave me not very much. And I felt for him something that Alessandro had never through love or hate felt for his. I felt . . . apathy" (180).

The little boy inside Neil, still locked in his room waiting for a pat on the head, has found freedom the only way possible: he must get on with his life and stop caring. In the next scene, he seems to be tightening his relationship with his girlfriend, and in the scene after that a pulmonary embolism kills his father. The death is a bit convenient, a deus ex machina that solves the problem of what Neil will do in the future. He is notably calm when he receives the news and makes certain that all the owners are contacted about their horses. Even Margaret, the loyal secretary, remarks that she much prefers working for the younger Griffon, and there is a sense that the elder Griffon will hardly be missed.

Those who do not offer love do not receive any. Neil, never having been offered any, has been crippled by it. Nevertheless, he has endured the suffering and has overcome it. He has come out better than might be expected, putting the lie to biological and psychological determinism. A man is free if he chooses to be free, but an act of will is necessary. His choice to offer Alessandro fatherly direction, a stern love whose lack has crippled Alessandro, will help set the world right. Neil will not die unloved. He will be loved as a surrogate father, as an employer, and, it is implied, as a husband. This is an essential quality of a good man in a Francis novel: he offers love. He may not be warm, but he still extends help to the unfortunate. That the blood shared by people has little or nothing to do with whether people might help each other may be seen as disturbing. These fathers and sons are anything but comforting. The message seems to be: You are not your father's son as much as you are what you make of yourself.

Long-Lost Family

Fathers who die before the hero gets to know them well are common in Francis. Also common is the individual estranged from his family. In one case, that of Philip Nore of *Reflex,* the hero knows nothing about his father, wants nothing to do with his family, but is given the chance to make contact. *Reflex* is one of Francis's best books. It is written crisply, the characters are consistently intriguing, and the plots intertwine with interesting twists. The hero is as darkly complex as Sid Halley. Nore is facing a number of choices with his life, and he is carefully refusing to choose. He is getting a bit too old to go on being busted up in horse races. He has hardly been setting the world on fire as a jockey anyway. He has thrown races on order from unscrupulous owners and trainers, but he has deceived himself as to his personal integrity by refusing to accept the bribes that would naturally follow from his well-acted tumbles from favored horses. He has been getting by as a jockey, but he knows that if he refuses to take such orders from his employers, he will lose his mounts and have no way to support himself. This is a situation he refuses to face up to. He will have to leave racing, either because he is going to be caught cheating or because of a serious injury. He knows he must plan for the inevitable, but he does not, and a man who does not make essential choices is no man. Says Nore: "I understood why I was as I was. I knew why I just drifted along, going where the tide took me. I knew why I was so passive, but I felt absolutely no desire to change things, to stamp about and insist on being master of my own fate."[11]

He is in a familial limbo, also, which may be the childhood cause of his adult passivity. He never knew his father, and his mother abandoned him to a succession of foster parents. Like Neil Griffon, it is remarkable that Nore has turned out as well as he did. Part of the credit must go to Duncan and Charlie, a gay couple who took in the twelve-year-old Nore. They patiently taught him photography. He was made to feel useful sweeping the floors and cleaning the darkroom. Eventually they trusted him to do most of their printing and called him their lab assistant, "A wizard, with a hypodermic" (33). Recounts Nore: "And I'd suck the tiny amounts accurately into the syringe and add them to the developer, and feel as if I were perhaps of some use in the world after all" (33). Later Nore describes the couple: "I thought of Duncan and Charlie who had hugged and kissed and loved each other all around me for three years. . . . Charlie, to me, had been father, uncle, guardian, all in one. Duncan had been chatty and quarrelsome and very good company, and neither of them had tried to teach me their way" (112). Duncan left for someone else, however: "Charlie's grief had been white-faced and desperately deep. He had put his arm around my shoulders and hugged me, and wept; and I'd wept for Charlie's unhappiness" (113).

Within a week, Philip's mother, "blowing in like a whirlwind," takes the boy away out of fear that the lonely Charlie might take advantage of him, though the way she says it indicates that Charlie does not think so. Philip tells him he does not want to go, but the fatherly man helps him by saying his mother is right and later by writing that Philip will soon get over missing him. Charlie takes two hundred sleeping pills, leaving a will that gives Philip all his darkroom equipment and a letter: " 'Look after your mother,' he wrote. 'I think she's sick. Keep on taking photographs, you already have the eye. You'll be all right, boy. So long now. Charlie' " (113). Even in his dying, he tries to overcome Philip's feeling of inadequacy. Years later,

Philip feels Charlie looking over his shoulder when he tapes the words "Copyright Philip Nore" on the back of his photographs (158), and he remembers Charlie teaching him how to mix the light from filters for color developing (182).

Nore's biological family is nearly a total loss, however, with a slight, though important, comparison drawn between the closeness of the dead photographer George Millace, his son Steve, and his wife. George's son would never belittle him, though George was "widely disliked" (24), and in subsequent scenes the closeness of this family is revealed in Steve's concern for his mother and her fear for Steve. By contrast, Nore does not know anything about his father. All he knows about his mother is a pastiche of memories, usually of her going out the door, and the suspicion that she died of heroin addiction. His search into his family history begins when he is summoned by his grandmother through her solicitor, Jeremy. "I had never met my grandmother," says Philip, "and I didn't want to, dying or dead. I didn't approve of deathbed repentances, last-minute insurances at the gates of hell. It was too damned late" (13–14). He relents, however, mostly on the principle that there is no reason to mimic her "stony rejection" (14).

Lavinia Nore is nastily triumphant when he shows up at the nursing home. She assumes he is after the hundred thousand pounds she intends to offer him to find his sister, a sister he did not know existed. "No one's idea of a sweet little pink-cheeked grannie" (15), she does not even know (and does not care) if her daughter, Philip's mother, is dead. Philip is not certain himself. Lavinia is clearly the distaff image of old Griffon in *Bonecrack:* tough as nails, cold, cynical, and cruel. But Philip is not as intimidated by her as Neil is of his father. When the old woman says that Philip's flippancy is disgraceful, he dishes back a good chunk of what she is dishing out. "Your behavior since my birth . . . gives you no right to say so," he says. ". . . She stared at me darkly in a daunting mixture of fury and ferocity. I saw, in that expression, what my poor young mother had had to face, and felt a great uprush of sympathy for the feckless butterfly who'd borne me" (17). He remembers his mother's being ejected from Lavinia's house when she tried to introduce little Philip to his grandmother and then the succession of married friends of his mother who took him in. "Never ill-treated, nor . . . ever, in the end, totally rejected . . . ," explains Philip, "it was an extraordinary, disorienting and rootless existence from which I emerged at twelve . . . able to do almost any job around the house and unable to love" (18). The longer stay with

Charlie and Duncan taught him something about love and gave him a profession, but when he was eighteen, the cards and presents his mother usually sent on holidays stopped coming, and he presumed her dead.

His feelings toward his mother are a sad mixture of pity and fantasy, which likely conceal the resentment he feels for having been shuffled about. Whatever anger he had toward his mother is now directed toward his grandmother. He remembers his mother as "full of flutter and laughter and gushing thanks. . . . She was, even to my eyes, deliciously pretty, to the extent that people hugged her and indulged her and lit up when she was around" (18). She was a poor butterfly—pretty and delicate and doomed. What Philip does not say, perhaps cannot say, is that she was directly responsible for his pathetic childhood. The grandmother may be indirectly responsible and should be held accountable, but it is the mother who is obviously primarily to blame, and Philip does not hold her culpable.

Lavinia wishes to leave her estate to Philip's sister, Amanda. Three detectives have failed to find her. Philip bluntly says he will not look for her. The reward means nothing to him. Later, however, Jeremy reappears with an offer Philip cannot refuse. "Do you know who your father is?" he asks. A long silence passes. Philip resists: "I don't want to get tangled up in a family I don't feel I belong to. I don't like their threads falling over me like a web" (53). The solicitor offers the files of the detectives, but Philip tells him to do his own dirty work. The solicitor smiles. "The dirty work was done about thirty years ago, wasn't it? Before either of us was born. This is just the muck floating back on the tide" (53–54). This remark is an interesting one; it seems to remove any of the blame for what has happened from Philip and seems to imply the possibility that one of Philip's problems is a feeling that he was somehow responsible, just as children often blame themselves for their parents' divorce.

Philip is changing. The rediscovery of a family is irritating because it is forcing him to take action. Once always passive, he is now being forced to choose, to take responsibility for his life. In the next scene, he suddenly tells an unethical trainer and owner that he will not throw a race. He knows the possible consequences—he may be fired—but the refusal "forced its way out, like water through a new spring." "When had I changed . . . ," he muses, "and how could it have happened without my noticing? I didn't know. I just had the sense of having already traveled too far not to turn back. Too far down a road

I didn't want to go" (59). When he returns home, he begins to scan the files on his missing sister, an indication he is pulled in the direction of discovering who he is, even though he does no more about it for many pages.

The solicitor, however, reappears. Lavinia has offered to tell Philip not only why she rejected Caroline but also who his father is. He is angry at first. He does not like being manipulated. He denies he wants to know who his father is. The solicitor does not believe him: "You want to know. . . . It's human nature" (101). Jeremy goes on to say that after Philip has found Amanda that he could forget the whole thing, but Philip knows there is no turning back if he goes forward: "You couldn't forget . . . who your father was" (102). He tries to talk himself into it because the persistent solicitor will never leave him at peace, but this merely disguises his emotional need: "the mists around my birth were there for the parting. The cataclysm which had echoed like a storm receding over the horizon through my earliest memories could at last be explained and understood. . . . I might in the event detest the man who fathered me. I might be horrified. But Jeremy was right. Given the chance . . . one had to know" (102).

Before he can see Lavinia, however, Jeremy sends him to find out why his Uncle James, whom he has never met, has been disinherited. James greets him with the remark, "I thought Caroline had aborted you. . . . Mother said the child had been got rid of" (105). Later he reports that Lavinia used to refer to the unborn Philip as "Caroline's disgusting fetus" (107). James looks nothing like Philip's mother, and Philip takes an instant disliking to him. When James's "naturally camp, and unmistakeable" male lover comes through the kitchen door, the reason for the disinheritance is obvious. James will not be passing along the Nore genes. James is an interesting counterpoint to Charlie. There is a strong, deliberate taint in the description of James, as if Francis were playing an unhealthy homosexuality off against a healthy. Charlie, after all, is Nore's de facto father, who gave him love and self-worth. James, however, seems to have been damaged by the scenes that took place in his house when he was young and the bitterness of his mother, which possibly resulted in his choice of life-style.

When Philip locates his sister, he finds her as damaged as James. A member of a cult, Amanda is seen by Philip as "childlike," "not exactly" mentally retarded, "but in the old sense, simple. There was no life in her, no fun, no awakening of womanhood. Beside the average teenager she was like a sleepwalker" (217). In his first perusal of her

face, he sees no resemblance between her and him (216). He sees her
only because she has been trusted to leave the commune to sell pretty
stones on the street. "Poor Amanda," he calls her, and decides that
letting the old woman know the girl is alive will only succeed in
wrenching her from the only family she has ever known, the only
security.

Similarly, when Lavinia tells Philip about his father, there is not
much satisfaction. She is willing to talk about the man because she
feels that she must pass on her genes. "Death is pointless otherwise,"
she remarks, and Philip thinks that life itself is "pretty pointless": "One
woke up alive, and did what one could and died" (179). He then,
however, concedes perhaps that the point of life is for genes to go on
and remarks that her genes may go on through him. She does not like
that possibility and scornfully asks if he is afraid to know who his
father is. Philip is ambivalent: "I simply stood there, not answering,
wanting to know and not wanting, afraid and not afraid: in an absolute
muddle" (179). First she says how much Philip looks like his father,
and then she reveals the stunning truth: his father was Lavinia's lover;
he lived with her. Philip asks if he is still alive and his name. Lavinia
refuses: "He ruined my life. He bedded my seventeen-year-old daughter
under my own roof and he was after my money. That's the sort of
man your father was. The only favor I'll do you is not to tell you his
name. So be satisfied" (180). His reaction is less one of horror at his
own conception than of sympathy for the old woman. She has allowed
a misfortune to destroy not only her own life but the lives of all those
around her. The full ironic weight of a Greek tragedy has inexorably
rolled over the happiness of an entire family because of the understandable
reaction of the bitter old woman.

Where does this leave Philip? The Nores, who should give Philip
his identity, have given him nothing. He has clambered over the ruins
of their lives and found nothing. His search has salved some of his
wounds, but it has done so by proving to him how utterly alone he
is. A man must make himself. The individual must choose to be what
he values best. A man is what he does, not his name, and not his
heredity. Having a father will not make a man stop throwing horse
races or stop him from hiding in a profession that makes less and less
sense as he grows older. The fact that he is forced into the family
because the stubborn Lavinia puts him in her will and because he states
his intention of making certain Amanda never wants is inconsequential
by book's end. More important is the fact that in this search for his

family, he has discovered love with Clare and is developing a strong relationship with her, the kind of relationship he has previously avoided. She is part of the healing by encouraging him to become a professional photographer.

He meditates on his new life and seemingly contradicts the plot's thrust: "because of looking for Amanda I had now met a grandmother, an uncle, a sister. I knew something at least of my father. I had a feeling of origin that I hadn't had before. I had people. I had people like everyone else had. Not necessarily loving or praiseworthy or successful, but *there*. I hadn't wanted them, but now that I had them they sat quietly in my mind like foundation stones" (283). Because of the search, he has also visited some of the people who took care of him for short periods, including Samantha:

Because of looking for Amanda I had found Samantha, and with her a feeling of continuity, of belonging. I saw the pattern of my childhood in a different perspective, not as a chopped up kaleidoscope, but as a curve. I knew a place where I'd been, and a woman who'd known me, and they seemed to lead smoothly now towards Charlie.

I no longer floated on the tide.

I had roots. (283)

These passages have certain sentimental satisfactions, but in several respects, they disregard the plot line of Philip's being stirred from his immobility. Everything still leads to Charlie, the only father Philip has ever had; the rest is merely detail. Philip has a deeper sense of his past, but it is hardly this sad past and this unfamilial family that has gotten him out of his emotional swamp. The roots he has discovered are no stronger than a waterlily's. Once he has found them, so what? When someone asks if he has family, he can say "Yes." He has been alone for so long he needs to feel that this new sense of his origins has made him able to face the future. What the reader has seen is a man making a series of choices that lead him to accept responsibility for himself. He chose to help Mrs. Millace and then chose to work out George Millace's blackmail puzzle and exposed the crimes. These had nothing to do with finding his roots. He chose to stop throwing races despite the possible ramifications. Again, this has nothing to do with his roots. He chose to embrace the relationship he has stumbled into with Clare; that her mother once cared for him is certainly not implied to be the reason for his interest in her. He also chose to search for Amanda and end his uneasiness with that aspect of his sense of self. Yet it is more his uneasiness with his overall sense of self that has precipitated his awakening than merely finding the wasteland of his family. He will no longer be able to fantasize that his life is their fault. The blame rests on him.

Looking at the village he lives in, he considers the future, no longer shying away: "I'd belonged in that village, been part of it, breathed its intrigues for seven years. Been happy, miserable, normal. It was what I'd called home. But now in mind and spirit I was leaving that place, and soon would in body as well. I would live somewhere else, with Clare. I would be a photographer. The future lay inside me; waiting, accepted. One day fairly soon I'd walk into it" (284). There will be no more hiding from himself. He walks down the hill "without any regrets" (284). It is a wise man who knows his own father but a wiser man who knows himself.

Filling Father's Shoes

With so many absent, dead, or emotionally absent fathers in Francis, Charlie is but one of the surrogate fathers that appears in the novels. Charles Roland has this sort of relationship with his son-in-law Sid Halley. Roland is tough in helping Sid face up to his situation, but he is also Sid's friend, helper, and role model. Roland is typical of the ideal fathers whom Francis shows to us as foster fathers, who contrast with the blood fathers. One of the most interesting and important qualities of these surrogates is their acting as a fire that tempers the steel of the heroes. They frequently are severe in their demands on the young man, but it is all to the good in turning boy into man. There might be a relationship between this harshness and the recurrent inability of the heroes to express feeling, but even this—though its liabilities are shown—is a traditional quality of manliness. Roland puts Sid through much humiliation in *Odds Against*. Sid's "guvnor" is also described as a disciplinarian when Sid was learning to ride. Paul Ekaterin, Tim's uncle in *Banker,* makes his nephew work his way up in the company, despite the envious suspicions that the boss's nephew is getting special treatment. Paul holds nothing against Tim for his father's dissolute waste of his inheritance, but he also makes Tim prove himself, giving him no special favors.

This steeling of the heroes is necessary in making them capable of withstanding the pressures that the hero of a thriller must endure and is clearly an important part of the father's role. Yet there is only a slight difference between making steel that holds a fine edge and making steel that is too brittle to be useful. The fathers often seem unnecessarily cruel. Kelly Hughes, the unjustly accused jockey of *Enquiry,* has both parents alive, but they are no emotional support for him. His mother writes that she knows Kelly denies having thrown a race, but he should not come home as they are painting his room for Aunt Myfanwy to live in, and they never really approved of his becoming a jockey. She writes: "I don't like to say it but you have disgraced us son, there's horrid gossip it is going into the village now, everyone whispering, your loving mother."[12] His father is worse. Writing so hard the ballpoint had almost dug through the paper, he begins: "You're a damned disgrace boy. . . . They wouldn't of warned you off if you didn't do it. Not lords and such" (96). Kelly then tells us, "He hadn't signed it. He wouldn't know how to, we had so little affection for each other. He had despised me from childhood for liking school. . . . [My family] had rigid minds. It was doubtful now if they would ever be pleased with me, whatever I did. . . . You couldn't take aspirins for that sort of pain. It stayed there, sticking in knives" (97).

More is going on with these situations than merely giving the hero another cross to bear. Making his heroes parentless contributes to their aloneness. The hero must be willing to attack an evil on his own (or with a few helpers, but he is always the leader). That he does so makes him distinct in a world in which most other people find it easier to look the other way. It also means he will face serious resistance since evil is used to getting its way. But as the hero, he will have the strength not only to face it alone but even to carry others who are not strong enough alone. Second, however, and most important, by cutting off his hero from conventional family supports, the example of a manly father or the sustaining love of a close family, Francis places the full responsibility for behavior upon the individual. A man can choose to be courageous if there is any courage in him. A man can choose to be loving and sympathetic if he wants to. The only limits are physical realities. While many of Francis's secondary characters might seem to imply that a man either has "the right stuff" or does not—with the hero not being too judgmental about those who do not—there are often acts of courage, small though tough ones, coming from weak characters. Who could be weaker than Jonah Dereham's alcoholic brother, Crispin, in *Knockdown?* Yet in the last scene, Crispin has taken a remarkable, though ironically futile, step toward recovery. There are several similar instances throughout the novels. The hero frequently does not know what he has in him, and force usually elicits fortitude. The message seems to be that a man is always alone, that in his loneliness he may reach out to other people and these others may love him and help him in his search for himself, but ultimately it is irrelevant to the quest for the inner self what name one carries or whether one's father or mother or children or wife is heartless or loving. When a man faces fear, he stares into a mirror.

Chapter Four
Men and Women
Manhood Without Machismo

The history of the hard-boiled detective novel is largely the history of a masculine entertainment based on values traditionally ascribed to the ideal man: integrity, incorruptibility, sexual attractiveness, and the ability to engage in combat without fear of death or pain. The detective is usually in the mold of Sir Walter Scott's Ivanhoe—not a wealthy knight, willing to champion the downtrodden even when not fully recovered from his own wounds, and the subject of the affections of both Rowena and the dark-haired Rebecca. Chandler made the knightly connection comically obvious in *Farewell My Lovely* when Philip Marlowe seeks "little Velma" who is masquerading as Helen "Grayle." With these roots in the chivalric romance—the intent of which was to a great extent the education of noble men—it is not surprising that the hard-boiled novel has generally lacked female heroes. There have been interesting attempts to adapt this distinctly male form of literature in this way, but the result has generally been parodistic and not popular in any significant way.[1] "Duking it out" with opponents has rarely been approved behavior for little girls though often sanctioned and encouraged for boys, and on the surface, at least, the idea of a hard-boiled female hero seems as grotesque as that of a woman boxer.[2] What sort of hard-boiled hero doesn't get thumped only to deliver righteous thumpery in return?

Therefore the hard-boiled novel often generates women characters who alienate readers by being stereotypes of the incompetent virgin, the good-hearted whore, and the demon-woman. In the first case, the woman is an innocent victim who needs protection from a man and lacks the brains or the toughness to get out of her bad situation. This kind of woman is always tripping when someone chases her or pathetically insists on the guiltlessness of her reprobate husband, father, or son. In the second situation, the woman is a blowsy and inept slut with one foot in the grave and ten fingers on a bottle of whiskey. She has been

burned out as a human being for years, often as the result of endless
buffeting largely her own fault. A typical example is Jessie Florian in
Chandler's *Farewell My Lovely*. Psychopathic and incredibly and blatantly
sexy, the demon-woman or witch shows up fairly regularly in the hard-
boiled novel. This latter-day version of John Keats's "La Belle Dame
Sans Merci" has one of her most famous appearances as Charlotte
Manning, who gets blasted away by Mike Hammer in *I, the Jury* while
trying to distract him by peeling her clothes. Velma Grayle of *Farewell
My Lovely* is also such a woman, as is Brigid O'Shaughnessy of *The
Maltese Falcon*. A strong correlation between the demon-witch's appearances and the fear of women usurping their roles might be doc-
umented by reference to social changes occurring at the time; "La Belle
Dame sans merci hath thee in thrall!" crops up in certain times to
reverberate as a line of horror.

Dick Francis began writing his novels in the early sixties, and they
have steadily appeared through two decades of significant change in the
roles of men and women. Francis is a man of relatively traditional
values. He varies the hard-boiled formula, even emphasizing its moral
conflict. Therefore, one might expect to find signs that he is alarmed
by the changes in men's and women's roles. Francis, however, shows
extraordinary equanimity in this regard. His books give an impression
that, like his heroes, he is not easily disturbed by people who violate
social rules as long as they do not intrude themselves into the lives of
others. There is nothing in his books or interviews that does not show
the most admirably stable, pragmatic, and secure character. Further, he
tends to stick carefully to the middle ground in his writing. His violence
is wrenching and memorable but hardly excessive or inappropriate to
the context. No reviewers believe that Francis has gone too far or fallen
too short. He is as steady a writer as he was a rider. This partly
explains his popularity. As Marty Knepper points out, "Even persons
not enamored of the hard-boiled mystery genre are reading and enjoying
Francis' novels."[3] It also particularly explains his popularity among
women. The main character in *The Question of Max*, written by a
literature professor who is a feminist, admits losing interest in all
detective novels except Dick Francis's "because she liked him."[4] The
mention of Dick Francis generally draws notably favorable responses
from a far larger number of women than might be expected. He offends
neither feminists as a group, nor more traditional women; he is neither
too macho nor too liberated in books centered around male values.

Sophie Randolph

Knockdown's hero, Jonah Dereham, is a bloodstock agent; he engages in the purchase of horses for clients and receives a commission in return. Like all other Francis heroes, he has his problems even before the plot moves to a canter. A former jockey, he has (like Francis himself) a bad shoulder, which will dislocate at the slightest provocation, and he must wear an uncomfortable strap to prevent the problem. Single, he has been "married, repented, and divorced, and in no hurry to make another mistake."[5] He is an orphan whose comfortable life was shattered when his mother was killed in a riding accident, and his father died three months later from a blood clot. The glitter of his and his brother's young lives was exposed as having been founded on financial quicksand, and they were forced to leave school, destroying their chances for university. Jonah adjusted by becoming a jockey and then shifting to bloodstock. His business is successful but not notably so. His honesty prevents him from gouging indifferent wealthy buyers and squeezing sellers, although these are common practices in the bloodstock trade around him, and his refusal to cooperate leads to threats, arson, and other subsequent criminal violence. His particular cross to bear is his brother, Crispin, a surly alcoholic whose abuses Jonah endures patiently.

Into this emotional wasteland—of Crispin's snoring on the sofa, rising sick, and verbally abusing the only person who will put up with him—enters Sophie Randolph. Their meeting comes about quite literally by accident. Jonah has a small stable yard he uses to hold horses for shipment. Because he does not make enough to hire anyone to help him, the stable is a drag on his energies, and he does not use it often. One night at twelve-thirty, the scrape of a hoof on a hard surface awakens him. He knows instantly that one of the three horses waiting for conveyance out of Gatwick airport is loose. The stall of the most valuable horse is empty, and seventy-thousand-pounds-sterling's worth of uninsured horseflesh is "loose on the dangerous roads of Surrey" (25–27). If the horse gets hurt, Dereham is ruined. Because it is hard to find a horse at night by car, he saddles up an old steeplechaser and sets off in pursuit. The search, over nonracing terrain, has most of the tension of the long chase scene at the end of *Dead Cert,* and once again the prose comes alive as Francis gets man on horse. It ends in "a horrific screech of tyres, some wildly scything headlights, a sickening bang and a crash of breaking glass" (29). The horse has run into traffic and caused a collision. Unhurt, it flees toward Jonah, who catches it, leads it back to its box, and returns to the scene of the crash.

A Rover and MGB GT are the accident vehicles, the latter having the worse damage. Isolated by headlights, Jonah sees "all men, all on their feet. And one girl" (32). This tableau is the first sign that Sophie Randolph can stand on equal footing with any man. Jonah describes her: "The girl stood looking at the orange remains of an MGB GT which had buried itself nose first into the ditch. She wore a long dress of a soft floaty material, white with a delicate black pattern and silver threads glittering in the lights. She had silver shoes and silver-blonde hair which hung straight on her shoulders, and she was bleeding" (32). So far, her name is not known by Jonah; she remains "the girl" for four more pages. The description in its choice of words emphasizes femininity, the essential "girlness" of the stranger: "a long dress of soft floaty material." The repetition of "silver" is soothing. It also implies value, preciousness, and purity. Only the last clause is startling. The reader has been lulled in the music of a traditional "boy meets girl," only to be jolted by the incongruity of beauty bleeding. Jonah then notices that the men on the scene are not behaving protectively. Sophie is "in icy command of herself, as cool and silver as the moonlight." She does not appear as young as Jonah had first thought; she is not a "girl." The wording suggests that "silver" may also imply a blue-white coldness, playing one paragraph off against the other and signaling the superficially incongruous features that make up Sophie. Why aren't the men behaving as they traditionally should to an injured girl? The first vision—a wish perhaps? Jonah seeing what he has been educated to believe is the ideal woman?—is supplanted by the reality of wounds, a personality that repels help, and by age. She has "scarlet splashes down the front of the pretty dress" and an "oozing cut"; prettiness clashes with blood smears, the sign of an adult woman.

A Freudian theorist might note that a number of other women in Francis seem to be at the beginning of a transition when they are associated with an image of blood. Roberta Cranfield of *Enquiry* is disagreeable—in many ways much like Sophie: "Not my idea of a cuddly bedmate," says Kelly Hughes. "Too cold, too controlled, too proud" (120). Two pages later, however, he has begun to think of her as beautiful, and when she shows her first affection for him, after he has barely survived a murder attempt, her dress is stained with her blood. Alessia Cenci of *The Danger* is described as almost childlike, but when she finally opens up to Andrew about the humiliations of her captivity, she weeps and tells of how the kidnappers, while leaving her naked in a tent, gave her only napkins when she menstruated, making her beg for even those.[6] Finally, as Red Riding Hood's clothing has been associated by Freudians with the onset of womanhood, so also in *Risk* the giving of a red cloak to Hilary Pinlock is a psychological symbol of her loss of virginity and new-found freedom.

With Sophie Randolph, once more Francis is playing with the concept of external appearance in conflict with internal reality, as he does with his male characters who look too young to be in their occupation or too tall to be jockeys, and certainly he is working to make her a mixture of qualities so that she will not fall into one of several bins of stereotypical love interests. Although Sophie is, at best, secondary to most of the plot, Francis succeeds, and she becomes primary to Jonah's characterization. Sophie becomes a distinctive personality.

Jonah soon discovers that Sophie is resourceful. During a tirade by the Rover driver, she says she needs to go to the bathroom, and Jonah takes her to his home. Once there, after he discreetly leaves her and takes care of unsaddling his old steeplechaser, she bluntly and directly speaks, "What you can give me now . . is a large drink." He offers tea. She demands any other drink at all. When he admits he has no liquor in the house, she sinks to the chair "as if her knees had given way" and says, "You bloody fool," with her voice "a mixture of scorn, anger, and, surprisingly, despair." "You let your stupid horse out and it nearly kills me and now you can't even save me with a bloody drink" (34). The whole point of going to Jonah's house had nothing to do with the bathroom; she has been at a party and had a few drinks. If tested by the police, she may register enough alcohol to cause her to lose her license. If she could be proved to have drunk after the accident, then the breathalyzer results would be inconclusive. Jonah helps her by swishing water in one of Crispin's discarded bottles and succeeds in deceiving the police when they arrive.

Jonah watches the questioning that reveals her name, her age (thirty-two), and her occupation (air traffic controller). Jonah also observes that she states her age with "no feminine hesitation" and that the policeman's pen hovers for five seconds before writing down her profession. Jonah states this all rather matter of factly, and yet the reader can sense his interest in her. As she describes the accident, he muses: "I looked at the girl; at Sophie Randolph, unmarried, thirty-two, air traffic controller, a woman accustomed to working on equal terms among males, and I remembered her instinctive reaction to the men at the scene of the

crash: even in a crisis she repelled protective cosseting because in everyday
life she could not afford it" (36). Notice how the hesitation in the
first line shifts "the girl" to a woman and how the apparent coldness
he had earlier seen—her seeming harshness before he fakes the drink
for her—now becomes understandable in the context of her professional
situation. There is sensitivity in his judgment, the kind of sympathy
that makes a Francis hero one of the best men in his world. He does
not, for example, assume that only a manly woman would want a
man's job; he assumes that the job and its conditions have shaped her.
He implies that she has had to prove herself better than any man
merely to hold a job that many men can hold by a minimal performance.
There is also the implication (proved later) that Sophie has the ethic
of professionalism that Francis and his heroes admire so clearly. As
Jonah is undaunted by the obstacles in his professional life, so is Sophie.
As Jonah adheres to a strong sense of what constitutes proper behavior
in his profession, so does Sophie. In the next chapter, though injured,
she insists on returning to her flat to wait in boredom on the remote
possibility her telephone will ring and she will be requested (she is on
standby) to replace someone who is ill. "The steel in her character,"
says Jonah, "showed little spikes when I tried to persuade her to give
my number to the people who might call her out on stand-by" (49).
Professionalism is not always easy or instinctive, but, as Francis always
reveals, such intensity is all that stands between order and chaos.

At the end of the chapter, when she finally shows the beginning of
a smile and tersely says, "Thanks," the reader knows that this is the
beginning of an important relationship. In one brief chapter, a fully
rounded character, Sophie, has been gradually revealed. She is unique,
likable but not universally so, and, most important, interesting. That
Jonah shows interest in her reveals his own exceptional character, his
own lack of tired notions about women, and it broadens his character
considerably. By the next morning, after she sleeps in his bed (alone),
he describes her again in a pair of paragraphs that is similar to his
first observations of her. In the first paragraph, he emphasizes her
physical attractiveness, closing with the words, "mouth softly pink
without lipstick." Then he proceeds to discuss her seeming brusqueness:
"Her composure, I began to understand, was not aggressive. It was
just that she gave no one any chance to patronize or diminish her
because she was female. Understandable if some men didn't like it.
But her colleagues, I thought, must find it restful" (39). Not only is
this a softening of the initial reaction, playing appearance off against

reality, but it is also a further elaboration of the theme of professionalism. Her standoffishness does not allow sex to intrude into the workplace— hence its restful quality. Coping with stacked airplanes and sexual fantasies is more than any man should attempt. She does not allow herself to become a sex object. She has gone a bit too far with her defensiveness because it intrudes to some extent into nonprofessional situations, but it has been necessary on the job, and an unfortunate earlier relationship with a pilot may be as much responsible for coolness as any carryover from work. Note too that Jonah thinks it "understandable if *some* men didn't like it" (39; my italics). Not him, though. This is the beginning of a friendship, a partnership of equals. When she begins to relax with Jonah, to sense that he is not trying to underestimate her, she goes to what seems like an extraordinary measure for her, giving him something: an explanation of the accident that makes the Rover driver as responsible as the horse. He thanks her, they smile, "and all the possibilities suddenly rose up like question marks" (40).

When Francis goes on to show quite vividly the degradations of life in a household burdened with an alcoholic, he also shows Sophie's strong character as she sits through Crispin's insensitive insults. After spilling cornflakes, sugar, and rice on the floor, he eventually notices her and asks, "Who the bloody hell are you?" (41). He calls her "Jonah's bloody popsy" and calls Jonah "a lecherous bastard." He blames Jonah for his own drunkenness, demands money, and then loudly vomits in the back yard. The implacable Sophie's sole reaction is to clear her throat (43). She does not respond to Crispin's provocations in any other way. She does not show any signs of anger. Similarly, much later in the novel when Crispin assumes that if a woman is present, she will clean up the dishes, Sophie calmly smokes, seeing "no reason to do jobs she disliked . . . simply because she was female" (170). That her questions of Jonah reveal that she does not understand what it is like to live with a drunk is further proof of her steel backbone. Her composure is not because she knows what alcoholics are like.

Jonah falls instantly in love. He does not want her to leave for work and without thinking asks her to marry him. It is a joke. Or is it? She, unrattled, says, "Yes, I will" (50), turning the joke around. His attempt to startle her has startled him. He begins to think about her "every ten minutes or so." He tries to deny it is really love. It is not quite right for a controlled man like him to go through love at first sight: "A cool girl I had kissed once on the cheek. . . . One couldn't call it love. Recognition, perhaps" (52). Jonah is either playing coy with the reader or trying to deceive himself. Either way, his carefully managed emotional balance has been thrown off. When he visits her at her home, he discovers that part of her emotional control is founded on the death of a man who lived with her for four years. She was deeply in love with him and perhaps is intent upon not allowing herself to go through such heartbreak again for any man. When she and Jonah kiss, "It was more a matter of warmth than of kindling passions." He says, "I could feel the withdrawal lying in wait only a fraction below the surface, a tenseness in the muscles warning me how easily I could go too far" (73). He reins in his galloping emotions and settles for an evening of quiet conversation, something she obviously appreciates after having said, "Most men nowadays think dinner leads straight to bed" (73).

They do, of course, get to bed. Jonah's stables and part of his house are burned, and Sophie arrives not wearing the gold necklace that symbolizes her dead lover. They get drunk together. They visit Crispin in the hospital. Finally he asks to borrow her sofa, and she offers her bed. Even here Francis is surprising. The cliché of the cold woman whose ice is melted by the love of a "real" man does not happen in *Knockdown*. After "sedate" driving, a "sedate" dinner, and a "sedate" movie on her television.

she was also in a way sedate in bed. The inner composure persisted. She seemed to raise a mental eyebrow in amusement at the antics humans got up to. She was quiet, and passive.

On the other hand she left me in no doubt that I gave her pleasure; and what I gave, I got.

It was an intense, gentle love making. A matter of small movements, not gymnastics. Of exquisite lingering sensations. And done on her part also, without reservation. (118)

Although the third paragraph seems at first to contradict the first, in fact it shows how carefully Francis has deliberately made her character complex. It would not make sense for her to be wildly passionate after having spent years in control, and yet she is not without emotions. The shoulder harness Jonah wears even to bed is perhaps a parallel to her reserve; to remove it, even during sex—especially during sex—could cause too much pain.

Francis also surprises with the resolution of these conflicts, as the story becomes a boy meets girl, gets girl, and sort of keeps her. Jonah faces the reality of the situation:

I thought that probably I did love her, and would for a long time. I also guessed that however often I might ask her to marry me, in the end, she would not. The longer and better I knew her the more I realized that she was by nature truly solitary. Lovers she might take, but a bustling family life would be alien and disruptive. I understood why her four years with the pilot had been a success: it was because of his continual long absences, not in spite of them. I understood her lack of even the memory of inconsolable grief. His death had merely left her where she basically liked to be, which was alone. (160)

Later, as if to harden his resolve, he recalls reading that air traffic controllers have "the highest divorce rate on earth" (161). Sophie is on the scene when Jonah discovers the villain behind the corrupt horse dealing, and she helps him avoid hours of pain by twisting and yanking his dislocated shoulder back into the socket. This is the only time in the novel in which she overtly loses her composure. Only Jonah's insult about her courage ("God give me a woman of strength" [178]) provokes her to attempt reseating the bone, but it takes some persuasion to get her back to her normal controlled self. When the bone scrunches into its socket, she weeps. With her feelings finally spilling out, the predictable pattern would seem to be forming: emotionally in touch with herself, she will overcome her reticence, and they will live happily ever after. But Francis was in an ironic mood when he wrote *Knockdown*. The last scene in the novel, Crispin's death so soon after seeking help for his addiction, proves that. The feelings that Jonah has released in Sophie are too much for her to deal with, and instead of rushing forward into Jonah's arms, she retreats. Jonah remarks, "Solitude offered her refuge, healing, and rest. I didn't. I had brought her a car crash, a man with a pitchfork, a bone-setting and a murder. I'd offered an alcoholic brother, a half-burnt home and a snap engagement. None of it designed for the wellbeing of someone who needed the order and peace of an ivory control tower" (182).

Francis implies that they will continue their relationship, but it will remain much as it is. They will be intimate friends and lovers but will not get into a more traditional situation, like marriage. "A dose of Dereham every week . . . might be bad for the nerves," says Sophie, "but at least I'd know I was alive" (183). Jonah willingly accepts her conditions. To some extent, she has been freed from her emotional prison, but she is who she is and were she to become a warm-hearted housewife, she would not be the woman whom Jonah fell for. She has been wounded, it is true, but Jonah is not judgmental. He does not imply that Sophie is defective as either a woman or a human being. Love makes Jonah willing to accommodate his fantasies to reality. Perhaps those fantasies contributed to the breakup of his first marriage. Crispin's attitudes to women might imply that Jonah's environment instilled those values. If this is the case, then Sophie has saved Jonah from living in a dream world of domesticated women. In return, she has been freed from the shell created by the memory of her pilot and can begin to live again.

The Salvation of Love

Salvation through love is a recurrent motif that is much more blatant in other novels, with the most obvious example in *Rat Race*. Matt Shore, with a "flat, mat name," is a pilot for an air taxi firm that specializes in ferrying horse owners, trainers, and high-priced jockeys from track to track.[7] He has just taken on the job and knows very little about what these people do; nor is he interested. "As negative as wallpaper" (27), he therefore is out of touch with the Edenic world of horse racing (discussed in the next chapter). Shore is very much in the image of the hard-boiled detective with his loyal secretary, crummy office, and drab, lonely apartment. For the air firm, Honey, the owner's niece, types the letters, keeps the records, and is the "keystone which held up the arch" (51). She has also "never refused a good pilot yet" (52) and hovers about waiting for Matt to ask for sexual favors. When Honey offers herself, Matt refuses; she calls him an iceberg and predicts, "You'll thaw. One of these days" (91). She buys him groceries, and he says she is "not a bad guy" (99). The crew room for the firm for which he works "looked as if the paint and walls were coming up to their silver wedding. The linoleum had long passed the age of consent. Three of the four cheap armchairs looked as if they had still to reach puberty, but the springs on the fourth were so badly broken that it was more comfortable to sit on the floor" (45). Shore lives in a seedy camper that belongs to the company. It has a rented television, "teeth marks of bottle caps along the fitments," "greasy head marks on the wall above every seat," gray, stained upholstery, and "shabby pinups of superhuman mammalian development." "Tired green curtains had opened and shut on a thousand hangovers," Matt says, and "the flyblown mirror had stared back a lot of disillusion" (56). He describes himself as "still with a license and not much else" (8). It is easy to imagine these words coming out of the mouth of Mike Hammer or Sam Spade, though Matt means a pilot's license. His mental state is even worse than his life-style. His depression has carried him through six jobs as a pilot, each bringing his expectations lower. The latest is the worst: "Squabbling passengers and belligerent competitors and no discernable joy anywhere" (13). Matt feels outside of life, and what he sees looking in is nasty, brutish, and short.

It is nearly sixty pages into the novel before the cause of this emotional devastation is revealed. Married at nineteen, he has gone through a terrible divorce. His ex-wife, Susan, stuck him with "mountainous bills," got their house, and is still collecting a quarter of his income. In a passage reminiscent of Sid Halley's wretched breakup with Jenny, Matt describes his shell shock: "I didn't understand how love could curdle so abysmally: looking back, I still couldn't understand. We had screamed at each other: hit each other, intending to hurt. . . . Since then I had tried more or less deliberately not to feel anything for anybody. Not to get involved. To be private, and apart, and cold. An ice pack after the tempest" (57–58). To have been this shattered, Matt obviously believed in romantic love very deeply and has resolved never to let himself slide into it again. But that is wrong, Francis implies. The romantic element that is so much a part of Matt's character must be allowed to express itself, or it will turn sour and destroy his soul.

Nancy, the sister of jockey Colin Ross, saves him. She abruptly enters Matt's emotional swamp by mistaking him for his predecessor and asking for a purse she had left in the plane. He likes her looks but otherwise does not react to her. She drags him away from his plane, however, explains a few things about the track to him, and then observes that he thinks it is all a joke: "You're looking at this race meeting in the way I'd look at a lot of spiritualists. Disbelieving and a bit superior" (18). After a bomb in the airplane, a fight, and the deepening of the mystery, Matt accepts Colin's invitation to stay at his house overnight when the weather looks unpleasant. There he meets Midge, Nancy's twin sister, who is dying of leukemia. He gains a sense of Nancy's fear of losing Midge. Midge is facing her death better than Matt is dealing with his misfortune, and she becomes an example of how one ought to grab life and hold on. When Colin describes her illness, Matt says "Poor Midge." Colin responds "Poor all of us" (84). Though he may mean the three siblings, his response also implies that all people are basically in the same situation: life is merely on loan, and there are no assurances about when it will be repossessed. Colin and Matt, though healthy, could have been killed by the bomb in their plane, and Midge would have outlived them. They even speculate that Nancy, because she is a twin, might also come down with the disease (86–87). The message of this exchange is reminiscent of Strether Lambert's desperate words in Henry James's *The Ambassadors:* "Live! Live all you can! It's a mistake not to!"[8] Matt does not get the message, however. He relaxes eating roast chicken and thinks he has not "passed a more basically satisfying evening for many a long weary year" (81). The alarm, however, goes off in his head and warns him not to get involved. The Rosses have shown him how to live—even in the fact that Colin, like he, is divorced but has recovered from the emotional shock—but Matt retreats back into his quagmire. If anything, it looks even drearier.

On another occasion, the Rosses take him on a picnic, and despite seeing a moorhen and making the pessimistic observation that "all of nature had its pecking order. Everywhere, someone was the pecked" (103), he relaxes even more, especially when the girls kiss him on each cheek and get tangled up with him while riding in the small Aston Martin. Later Nancy asks Matt to comfort her. She has been thinking about Midge's illness. For the first time, Matt begins to believe he might be normal again, though it frightens him. "They could heal me, the Ross family, I thought. Their strength could heal me. If it would take nothing away from them. If I could be sure" (109). More important, he makes a small sacrifice for their sake. Nancy indirectly offers to be his girlfriend. He refuses, but not merely to keep himself wrapped up. He does not want to interfere with the family unity that helps each of them deal with Midge's imminent death. He is becoming part of the chain of human sympathy.

The final step in Matt's recovery is the desperate airborne chase in which he searches the sky for Nancy who is flying a plane rigged for an electrical failure. In order to save her, he risks his license, he violates the law, and he angers one of his passengers. Nonetheless, throughout the tense sequence of events, Matt is anxious, sweaty, and feeling. One of his passengers remarks that Matt has "no bloody nerves. . . . Not a bleeding nerve in his whole body" (143), but the reader knows different. The face may be glacial, but the ice is melting. He joyously greets Nancy when the plane is safe, grabbing her around the waist and swinging her in the air. She kisses him, and he kisses her: on his "own account" (144). Matt has a brief relapse as the excitement dies down. He comments on the homey, "familiar, cozy, undemanding, easy" feel of the Ross house, but he adds, "It was no good feeling I belonged there, because I didn't" (151). Soon, also, some of the bad luck in Matt's past comes to light, and the yellow press (along with a rival air taxi company) flings it in Nancy's face, causing Colin to change companies. Colin blames Matt for disrupting his family, and Nancy runs away to her old boyfriend, Chanter, a filthy and obnoxious painter who has not found out that the sixties have ended.

Waiting for four days to find out where Nancy is, Matt gives all the signs of being in love. He is jealous and miserable in a way much different from his deliberate freeze at the beginning of the novel: "Four wretched, dragging days," he comments. "Four endless, grinding nights" (184). Eventually, however, Nancy tells Midge that she did not run away with her old boyfriend; she had gotten the impression that Matt wanted to marry her and is now too humiliated to face Matt. Matt says, like a proper gentleman, that he had never considered marriage because of his impoverishment. Colin rebuts that it does not matter, and both he and Midge persuade Matt that he will join their family, not destroy it, by marrying Nancy. "She'd have to live on peanuts," says Matt. "For crying out loud," says Colin, "what does that matter? You can move in with us. We all want you. Midge wants you—and now, not some distant time when you think you can afford it. Time for us is now, this summer. There may not be much after this" (196). Matt stares his own death in the eye before he makes the final choice of once again embracing life. Bleeding from a knife wound, he thinks of "the girl I hadn't wanted to get involved with, who had melted a load of ice like an acetylene torch" (210). On the last page of the novel, Matt collapses from loss of blood. "Don't bloody die!" says Nancy, and the lightheaded Matt grins and asks, "Want a lodger?" passing out before he can propose. The last line is cutely ironic: "Everything drifted quietly away, and by the time I reached the ground I couldn't feel anything at all" (216). Of course, the reader knows this is not Matt's death scene (he has narrated his tale), and though he may be slipping into unconsciousness, he will come out of it, feeling life and risking the dangers of love in a way he had sworn to avoid.

Lord Grey and the Virginal Heroine

Another hero much like Matt Shore is the narrator of *Flying Finish*, Henry Grey, future earl of Creggan, amateur jockey and pilot, a man who is mired in his own coldness: "A repressed, quiet, 'good' little boy I had been, and a quiet, withdrawn, secretive man I had become. I was almost pathologically tidy and methodical, early for every appointment, controlled alike in behavior, handwriting, and sex. A prim dim nothing. . . . The fact that for some months now I had not felt in the least like that inside was confusing, and getting more so" (14–15). I have some reservations that a person like Henry could be so insightful about the nature of his own personality, especially when he is maladjusted. To have such precise self-knowledge would seem to imply the ability to take care of the problem, and Henry is clearly more confused than that, vacillating among his obligations as a lord, his interest in racing, and his skill as a pilot. The job he takes as an attendant to race horses shipped by air is plainly a temporary measure, acquired only to gain the freedom to make decisions about his life. In the passage above, he seems almost to think of himself in the third person, which might have been taken as a manifestation of his personality but is more likely the author borrowing Henry to tell the reader directly what the character is like.

Henry is plainly in emotional limbo. His family is trying to find him a suitable bride, a woman with the money to restore the earl of Creggan's fortunes and who might like the social stature of acquiring an old title and its remaining estates. Henry does all he can to avoid the dates arranged by his family, which only causes more pressure as he makes them apoplectic with desperate anger. Meantime, as an excellent amateur jockey, he feels the pressure to get his professional license. Amateurs may be tolerated in races in Britain, but a successful amateur is thought to be taking food out of the mouths of professionals' families and soon finds he is limited, as Henry is, to a specific number of rides per year. Henry also, on occasion, taxis people for a small airline, the owner of which is faced with a shortage of pilots and keeps asking Henry to take a full-time position.

Juggling these activities while flying from country to country with a load of race horses helps Henry avoid making a decision about his life and identity and simultaneously symbolizes the disorder in his mind. He only knows what he does not want—to be earl of Creggan—but will not commit himself to a choice. He tells his friend Simon, "I am not an anachronism. I'm Henry Grey, conceived and born, like everybody else, into this present world. Well, I insist on living in it. I am not going to be shoved off into an unreal playboy existence where my only function is to sire the next in line, which is what my parents want"

(54). Simon suggests he renounce his title, and Henry then begs the question with the irrelevant argument that the only reason to do this is to make himself eligible for election to the House of Commons, which he would not do because he has no interest in politics. It is a *non sequitur* he justifies by saying he wants people "to acknowledge that an earl is as good as the next man, and give him an equal chance" (54). He seems to be trying to shift the responsibility for his life to other people; he would not have a problem if others would accept him as he is. Yet Francis continually shows us that a man is what he does, not what he thinks he is. There is a wonderful, "No Exit" quality to Henry's riding in the cargo space of an airplane with several horses, the homicidal punk, Billy, and the aged, nearly deaf Alf.

Henry is rescued from this existential hell by love. This is typical of Francis novels, and though there might be exceptions, such as *Knockdown* and *Proof,* the situation in *Flying Finish* appears in various forms but is usually, even if only rudimentarily, there. In *Flying Finish,* the importance of the woman is clear from her first appearance. A blizzard strands the cargo plane in Milan. The pilot, Patrick, offers to take Henry to an Italian family he berths with when he is stranded. Although Henry is inclined to be alone, he accepts the offer rather than search for a hotel. They enter the airport, and Patrick introduces him to Gabriella: "I stood on the cool stone airport floor and felt as if I'd been struck by lightning: the world had tilted, the air was crackling, the gray February day blazed with light, and all because of a perfectly ordinary girl who sold souvenirs to tourists" (78–79). This is an extraordinary spasm of emotion not just for "prim dim" Henry but for any other Francis hero. The love relationships usually develop in a much more indirect way. Hard-boiled writers frequently use gruff exteriors to conceal deep sentimentality, but such guileless emotion, such ingenuous romance, is rare. Despite having to communicate in awkward French— she speaks no English, he no Italian—their relationship soars. Wanting to make certain it does not influence her, he does not tell her about his ancestry, but it matters only to him because she is as clearly smitten as he.

There are no prickles on Gabriella as there are on Sophie Randolph and Roberta Cranfield of *Enquiry,* but Gabriella is more representative of the typical Francis hero's love interest. She is serenely beautiful. Her face reminds Henry "of medieval Italian paintings," and "her expression, except when she smiled, was so wholly calm as to be almost unfriendly" (80). This emotional reserve she shares with Sophie and other Francis "leading ladies," as well as almost all of Francis's heroes, so it can be assumed that the author considers it a desirable trait, even though (mostly in the heroes) it can go too far. She is not used to impetuous emotions: "Each time she spoke and looked at me in a kaleidoscopic mixture of excitement, caution, and surprise, as if she too found falling helplessly in love with a complete stranger an overwhelming and almost frightening business" (82). Giving in to one's emotions is dangerous, for either men or women, and although no human being can succeed in controlling them completely, the ideal is always present in Francis's most admirable characters.

The love interest of the hero, as might be expected, also avoids the extremes of sexual behavior. The grittiness of the hero's loving a woman who has been too generous with her body (a prostitute, for example) is absent. There are numerous prostitutes with whom other hard-boiled detectives have affectionate relationships—supporting, though not approving, of the "profession"—but Francis avoids these situations. He has no prostitutes in his novels. There are a few women casual about sex, but they are usually minor characters (Patty in *For Kicks,* for example). Gail, of *Forfeit,* broadly hints to James Tyrone that she will not sit home alone if another attractive man is available, but this might be Tyrone reading his fantasies into her (he needs unattached sex because of his ill wife); later, whenever he calls, she cancels her previous engagements. At the same time, as the hero is nonjudgmental about sexual peccadillos, the hero's beloved is not a prude. She usually does not stave off sexual intimacy too long. When the time is right, she knows her own mind. Henry's plane has been grounded for a second day in Milan when he and Gabriella consummate their love in the back of a DC-4 cargo plane, and there is a clear implication that this step is necessary to confirm the validity of their "love at first sight." Henry says discreetly that at sex, "We were relieved to find that we suited each other perfectly" (93). The relief is clearly at not having been deceived by strong feeling.

Gabriella, however, is, if not a virgin (and there is no indication she is not), clearly virginal, and this is a recurring quality of Francis's women. Though not prudish (Gabriella helps smuggle birth control pills into Italy, where they are illegal), they are usually not very experienced. Sophie had had a long-term relationship with a pilot. Allie, in *High Stakes,* has had a poor experience with a boy at college and is afraid she will never enjoy sex, so she puts off Steven Scott for a while so as not to disappoint him. Neither is, of course, and by the end of the novel, she is fully involved with him. He, a detached maker of toys and puppeteer of his friends, is not only among friends and in love but has embraced his obligation as a horse owner to get to know his horses as fellow beings. Alan York's love, Kate Ellery-Penn, is also cool, having an "inexhaustible inner fire battened down tight under hatches" (*DC,* 41) from childhood by an Edwardian aunt and she is described as "unawakened" (136). In *Banker* Tim Ekaterin's love interest is married, but the two of them pristinely avoid adultery despite powerful feelings. In this case, Tim is even more restrained than she.

These virginal aspects of Francis heroines are reminiscent of the cliché of the motion picture heroine who is pure and inevitably bumbles into trouble in order to be rescued by her man. Francis fuzzies up the outline a bit by giving many of the heroines prenovel sexual experiences, a bit of prickliness in personality, and careers in traditional male occupations, but the outline is still frequently recognizable. The imperceptiveness of Gail in *Forfeit* and Elinor in *For Kicks* results in typical bumblings that increase the life-threatening danger to the heroes of those novels. The well-meaning female innocently blabs too much in both cases, and the villains instantly take advantage, at the cost of the hero's bones.

Another obvious virginal heroine is Alessia Cenci, the romantic interest of Andrew Douglas in *The Danger.* She is strong-willed enough to be a successful jockey; she has "not just courage, not just talent, but style" (98). She is nonetheless portrayed more like a schoolgirl, partly justified as the result of her temporary fragility of having been mentally raped by her kidnappers. A psychological dependency on the hero is often part of the pattern of Francis's female characters. Abandoned in only a raincoat after the ransom exchange, Alessia is carried by Andrew and described in these words: "She had the body of a child, I thought. Smooth skin, slender limbs, breasts like buds. . . . She had been light to carry in the car, and I'd lain her on her side on the rear seat, her knees bent, her curly head resting on my rolled up jacket" (65). Later she goes through a period of recovery in England with a substitute mother (her mother is dead) in which she has to redevelop her confidence on horses, and Andrew takes on a fatherly role of amateur psychiatrist, confessor, and comforter while carefully making certain he does not violate her trust by rushing her into a relationship with him: "She needed to grow safely back to independence and I to find a strong and equal partner. The clinging with the clung-to wasn't a good proposition for long-term success" (271). When Alessia assists another woman whose boy has been kidnapped, she seems to be well on the road to recovery, suffering only a small relapse when she rides her first race since the kidnapping and loses. Douglas is there, however, always propping her up when she stumbles, yet keeping his deepening love for her hidden behind his cool exterior, the emotionally reticent character of a typical Francis hero.

When he finally does make his move, she refuses his arm around her waist and demurely looks not at him but at the track (311). After they spend a day driving around Washington, D.C., together, she reveals her romantic past, which is virginal though not pure: "I don't seem to want . . since the kidnap . . . I've thought of kissing . . of love . . . and I'm dead. . . . I went out with Lorenzo once or twice and he wanted to kiss me. . . . I did love someone passionately once, years ago, when I was eighteen. It didn't last beyond summer. . . . We both simply grew up" (317–18). Her explanation provokes Andrew's confession of love and once again we have a hero saved from his inability to express his emotional self: "it was I, really, who wanted to be enfolded and cherished and loved" (318). There is also, however, a reluctant acceptance of the fact that he cannot possess her. When she is riding Brunelleschi in the Washington International, he thinks: "I felt . . . a sense of being no part of her real life. She lived most intensely there, on a horse, where her skill filled her. All I could ever be to her as a lover, I thought, was a support: and I would settle for that, if she would come to it" (321). She does come to it, of course, saying she loves him after she wins the race and then (during Douglas's kidnapping) blurting to the American police that she did not know she loved Douglas like she did and regretted refusing his offer to go to bed. The future, after the end of the novel, is transparent.

Sexual Restraint

It is in this virginal quality of Francis heroines that he begins to reveal a set of more traditional values for women than one might superficially expect from their independence and nontraditional occupations. Francis heroines establish a certain equality with men by holding important professional positions (jockey, television newswoman, a caterer, a musician), by having had at least some sexual experience, and by not seeking to establish themselves in a traditional dependent housewife's role. When Francis shows us a good marriage, such as Edward and "Charlie" Link's in *Smokescreen,* he shows a relationship that is not without its shaky moments (the Links must deal with a retarded daughter and "the onslaughts of success and prosperity" [20] that come with his being a movie star) but that has evolved into the give and take of a partnership. A partnership is what Francis's main women characters seek, with always a "room of her own," a place, such as in the case of Alessia on horseback, where the man cannot intrude. Men can never possess them in all ways. On the other hand, they are more virginal than experienced, they usually do not contribute significantly to the solution of the mystery, and they tend to be extremely dependent on the hero for protection, rescue, and the soothing of psychic wounds.

Alessia, for example, is totally humiliated and degraded by the experience of being kidnapped. She even suffers from identification with her kidnapper and cannot help having confused feelings about the prospect of his capture; she wants revenge but does not want Douglas hurt. She is totally dependent on him for her return to normality, refusing the help of a psychiatrist when Douglas suggests it. Even when she goes to Popsy's stables in England to recover, the stern woman trainer has little effect on Alessia, and it is obviously Douglas who shakes her free from her nightmares. In *High Stakes,* Alexandra Ward gleefully participates in Steven Scott's scheme, with several of his friends, to undo the criminals. In fact, there is a joyful camaraderie in his friends' taking roles to deceive the bad guys. Although Scott is clearly the dominant character, his plucky lieutenants make him seem less of a lone wolf than most other Francis heroes. In the exciting final scene in which Scott gives his four unlikely friends (Bert the Communist, Charlie the merchant banker, Owen the Welsh servant, and Allie) equal shares in the horse Energise, they all watch it run. Allie is plainly an equal to the other friends; however, they all remain Scott's aides throughout the novel, not his partners. It is he who gives them the horse. It is he who devises the plan. In the imagery often repeated in the novel, Scott is like the operator of his best-selling toy; he turns the handle, and the gears start the carousels, clowns, and other parts moving. Charlie likens the moving toys to the criminals, but the friends could easily be likened to the gears. Similarly, Joanna in *Nerve* assists Rob Finn in implementing his plan for righteous revenge on Maurice Kemp-Lore. She impersonates a tipster on the telephone and helps Finn set up the cottage trap, but she is strictly following Finn's instructions.

Because women are usually important only in the romantic subplot, it is unusual for them to be physically injured—shot, beaten, or tortured. An exception is Gabriella in *Flying Finish,* who is shot on a street while she and Henry are running to catch a tram. About the only function Gabriella has played in trying to solve the mystery, however, is having done a little legwork on the missing Simon and acting as Henry's translator. Except for the love affair, she plays a role no larger than the student Stephen in *Trial Run* who translates for Randall Drew in Moscow. It is a trifle unusual, given the love interest, that *Flying Finish* ends without certainty that Gabriella has recovered. Henry, still in the plane for home, says only, "Yet in a sort of exhausted peace I found myself believing that as against all probability I had survived the night, so had Gabriella . . . that away back in Milan she would be breathing safely through her damaged lung. I had to believe it. Nothing else would do" (252). He then describes the landing. It is a clever way to close, avoiding the cliché of the inevitable tearful reunion and happiness ever after. But also it is vaguely disturbing; the reader can imagine Henry finding out the worst and being thrown back into his emotional shell by the devastation of losing Gabriella.

A few women are placed in life-threatening situations from which the hero saves them. In *Enquiry* Roberta and her mother are held hostage by a madwoman with a long filleting knife. In a tense and then explosive scene, Kelly Hughes gradually turns the madwoman's anger against him, despite his crutches, and desperately struggles with her as she tries to kill him. "Her strength," he says, "made a joke of mine" (194), and it eventually takes three men to restrain her until the doctor arrives with a sedative. Jonathan Derry's wife, Sarah, and their friend, Donna, are also held hostage by the supremely evil thug, Angelo Gilbert, in *Twice Shy*. He threatens Jonathan: "any funny stuff and your little wifey will keep the plastic surgery business in work for years. Starting with her nice white teeth, creep."[9] That does not make Jonathan stay away from "funny stuff," and like any other Francis hero, he sets in motion a scheme that undoes the gangsters. When he arrives to rescue his wife and Donna, they have been tied with rubber straps to chairs for a long time, but except for the mental strain (which is considerable), they are unharmed. Angelo and his cousin, Eddy, released them when they needed the bathroom and fed them twice. They also forced Sarah to cook, but they did not beat the women or sexually abuse them. This latter question hangs in the air when Donna sobs, "It's been awful. *Awful*. You've no idea," and Jonathan asks, "They didn't . . .?" Sarah says no, "They just sneered" (142). Like Alessia Cenci, these women have been verbally abused, humiliated, and confined, but they have not been physically violated. An exception occurs in *Banker* when Ginnie Knowles, the teenage daughter of a horse trainer, has her skull bashed in when she stumbles across the reason that horses have been delivering deformed foals, but it happens quickly and there is no sexual element in it (198). Later the hero tells her father that she died without ever knowing what hit her, perhaps an effort to comfort. Another exception is *In the Frame,* which begins with the murder of Regina. She was murdered when she came home at an unusual time and found her house being robbed. Dispatched by a blow to the head from a bronze statuette of a horse, she may have raised her hands in supplication, but there was no toying with her (12). The heaviness of the statue indicates that her end was quick, and the matter-of-fact initial description of her body lying in a pool of her own urine is free of the Baudelaireian eroticism frequently used in similar novelistic situations.

Given the context of our times and the blurring of sex and violence that takes place not just in hard-boiled thrillers but in science fiction, westerns, motion pictures of all sorts, and especially horror fiction, a reader who is repulsed by the implicit titillations of such violence can only be delighted by Francis's avoidance of it. So powerful are his descriptions of the violence men do to men that Francis has provoked the word *sadistic* from reviewers, but he draws the line at sexual violence. This is another example of the essentially moral intention of his entertainments. To describe sexual violence or to depict sexual violence with the intention of realistically portraying its brutality may incite the very cruelties it purports to expose or at the very least cause readers or viewers to become even more indifferent to them than they already are from the bombardments of real violence reported by the media. It may perhaps be naive to assume that there is less sexuality in a man beating a man, but Francis is not interested in the psychology of his criminals, so he ignores this aspect. The immediate sexuality of a man overpowering a woman, however, is more obvious, and he reveals his gentlemanly reserve by not including tortures other than the psychological. It is also, I suspect, a reason he remains consistently popular, given the assumption that mysteries in general are sought exactly because they provide a mythology of right rationally and inevitably triumphing over wrong.

Sexual activity in general is delicately dealt with. The narrators are frank about their attractions to women, and each is frank about desiring to take his beloved to bed. Francis does not write explicitly about the sex act itself, though he does not completely draw the veil. There are only general descriptions of what the act was like and a few evocative details. Although the narrator is never an innocent in sex, he often seems to become embarrassed by his own desires and describes them in a convoluted way. Francis has no heroes who are as sexually dissolute as, for example, the detective is occasionally implied to be in Dashiell Hammett's *The Dain Curse*. Mickey Spillane's Mike Hammer often seems to turn down women in order to humiliate them, but he is open to many offers. On the other hand, Francis is not unsophisticated. *Tasteful* is the word for Francis's handling of sexuality. Although there may be offstage rutting and a few instances of sexual perversity, the sexual act he gently shows is usually one of love between a man and a woman—though I might also include the rhapsodic mating of Sand-castle with a mare in *Banker*. The narrator describes it as "a copulation of thrust and grandeur, of vigor and pleasure, not without tenderness: remarkably touching" (147).

Philip Nore's account of his adoptive homosexual parents in *Reflex* is so sympathetic that gayness hardly seems to qualify as perversion. In *Enquiry,* however, Kelly Hughes discovers that Lord Gowery has been blackmailed into framing Hughes for fixing a race because of his predilection for sadomasochism. Gowery belongs to a secret London club where people of similar interests meet for those purposes. Lord Ferth awkwardly reveals the facts to Hughes: "He told me. . . . He told me that he has . . . he suffers from . . . unacceptable sexual appetites. Not homosexual. Perhaps that would have been better . . . simpler" (156). Ferth finally sputters out the word "Flagellation," and Hughes shocks him by his amusement: "That old thing! [says Hughes]. The English disease. Shades of Fanny Hill. . . . You must have read their coy little advertisements? . . . I don't actually understand why anyone should get fixated on leather or rubber or hair, or on those instead of anything else. Why not coal, for instance—or silk?" (156). Lord Ferth says Hughes takes it too coolly, and Hughes replies, "Live and let live. . . . they're not harming anyone." Even after Ferth's protestations that it is incredible for a racing steward to be so interested and that no one could respect Gowery any more, that "one can't like him," Hughes replies that these people do less harm than those who abuse children and finally concludes that Gowery has been "unlucky, in more ways than one" (157). There is a clear implication of "There, but for the grace of God, go I." Lord Gowery is an object of pity, not revulsion. That a villain would exploit Gowery's problem is evil, but the perversion itself is a misfortune more than a crime. This particular instance of sexual abnormality is notable as the only one directly described, and yet it is not handled with hysteria. As Francis balances the realities of the modern woman with the more traditional ideal of woman, he balances the realities of sexual variety against the ideal of male and female finding their perfect Platonic soul mates. This rational sense of balance is one important reason he usually seems neither pristine nor prurient.

Tim Ekaterin

Sometimes Francis's heroes seem almost too fastidiously romantic. They look for love, not mere pleasure, and they do not allow themselves to yield to an obvious opportunity when it might interfere with the ultimate achievement of true love. Despite his love for Alessia, Andrew Douglas restrains himself so that her dependency on him does not result in an artificial relationship. The almost annoying, extreme example of such restraint is Tim Ekaterin's relationship with Judith. In *Banker,* Gordon Michaels is Tim's supervisor at the bank founded by Tim's great-grandfather. The novel begins with Gordon standing in a fountain while suffering a hallucinatory attack brought on by an overdose of a drug for his Parkinson's disease. Although drugs and healing are a recurrent element of the plot, the eeriness of this opening has nothing to do with the skullduggery later discovered. Gordon, however, is married to Judith, and when Tim takes him home, he faces once again his attraction for her: "Judith Michaels, somewhere in the later thirties, was a brown-haired woman in whom the life-force flowed strongly and with whom I could easily have fallen in love. I'd met her several times . . . and had been conscious freshly each time of the warmth and glamour that were as normal to her as breathing" (10). In fact, this is either deceptive, or Tim is trying to suppress his own feelings. He is clearly already in love. He also says that entangling oneself with the boss's wife is hardly "best for one's prospects" (10), but this proves to be a remark to cover the fact that Tim would not betray a friend and colleague, never mind that he is the boss. That he happily takes Gordon's place while he recovers is more than just delight in getting increased responsibility; it is emblematic of his desire to replace Gordon in both the professional and personal spheres.

The gentleman's code by which Tim lives can be contrasted with the behavior of John, another colleague, who is miffed that Tim was selected over him to replace Gordon. John fancies himself a Lothario.

He has "difficulty in fitting the full lurid details of his sexual adventures" into his supervisor's trips to the restroom. Says Tim: "Neither Alec [another banker] nor I ever believed John's sagas, but at least Alec found them funny, which I didn't. There was an element lurking there of a hatred of women, as if every boasted possession (real or not) was a statement of spite. He didn't actually use the word possession. He said 'made' and 'screwed' and 'had it off with the little cow.' I didn't like him much and he thought me a prig" (24). Tim to some extent (like most other Francis heroes) is a bit of a prig, though he is willing to admit to his mother that he has slept with several "perfectly presentable girls" (168). He tells her he is choosy, but he is nonetheless stiff-necked, partly because he is old-fashioned in clutching on to the vision of the ideal woman as a creature to be placed on a marble pedestal (and only the perfect woman should be his wife) but mainly because he holds such extraordinary control over his emotions. Sid Halley and other Francis jockeys become expert at concealing physical pain so that they do not have rides cancelled. This control spreads also to the emotions, and the jockeys pay for it. Tim perhaps is afraid of losing control because of the alcoholism that impoverished his father, so he becomes, as the narrator often becomes in Francis, a contradictory mixture of pragmatic acceptance of the weaknesses that drive others (with absolute dominion over his own) and an idolator at the altar of pure womanhood. A Francis hero does not "make it" with a woman; he "makes love." Tim looks upon his love with a charming romantic traditional innocence, yet he also is "puzzled" why there are "so few women among the managers." Why "puzzled"? Isn't it obvious that banking has been male dominated? Gordon says the conventional "few women wanted to commit their whole lives to making money," and John makes the contemptuous observation that women prefer to spend money rather than earn it (61). Tim is an interesting clash of attitudes toward women: his basic conservatism being resisted in a way that makes it often seem he protests too loudly.

Another woman enters the picture when Tim is introduced at Ascot to Pen Warner, a "worthy," "well-intentioned" pharmacist with "the long, sad knowledge of human frailty" in her eyes (33). Pen could easily turn out to be like many another unusual love interest for the hero but instead becomes more of the frowsy, tough, independent woman, like Popsy in *The Danger,* who is worldly wise, older, a reliable comrade, but no one's idea of romance. She eventually contributes to unraveling the mystery because of her chemical knowledge. There are many instances in this novel when Tim seems to pal around with her to cover his interest in Judith and when it also seems that he will soon come to accept the situation and end his loneliness by deepening his relationship with Pen. It never happens. They walk, they talk, he gives her a kite at Christmas that everyone has fun with, but he does not get closer.

He covers his flirtations with Judith at Ascot by pretending they are jokes, and when they talk privately on the balcony the chitchat gradually develops into the following exchange:

[Tim says,] "On a day like this one could fall in love."
"Yes, one could." She was reading her race card overintently. "But should one?"
After a pause, I said, "No, I don't think so."
"Nor do I." She looked up with seriousness and understanding and with a smile in her mind. "I've known you six years."
"I haven't been faithful," I said.
She laughed and the moment passed, but the declaration had quite plainly been made and in a way accepted. (36–37)

It is a relief to know that Tim has not taken a vow of chastity because of his secret love, yet what she thinks about this is enigmatic. She could be a woman flattered by attentions she has no real intention of returning. Yet the reader is led to believe that this is a moment similar to Henry's thunderstruck meeting with Gabriella. If it is—and only Tim's interpretation is given at this point—then Judith is extremely placid about it.

During a three-day visit to the Michaelses' home, Tim has the best Christmas since he was a boy. He sees how efficiently Judith cares for the home, sees her in an unrevealing dressing gown, and kisses her "uninhibitedly" under the mistletoe, which Gordon and everyone else takes for good spirits. The day after Christmas, he takes Judith to her mother's grave. Gordon does not go with them, as he considers the visits "too sentimental," and it turns out the cemetery is in the neighborhood of Tim's flat. As they talk by the gate, he thinks, "I wanted very much to go that last half mile: that short distance on wheels, that far journey in commitment. My body tingled . . . rippled . . . from hunger, and I found myself physically clenching my back teeth" (108). When she asks what he is thinking, he blurts out that she knows what he is thinking and for that reason they are going back to her house immediately. Interestingly she sighs and says, "Yes, I suppose we must." The *suppose* catches him by surprise, and she admits she has been tempted, as at Ascot. He then says that even though they now have the time and opportunity, they will do nothing. "Why do we *care?*" she explodes. "Why don't we just get in your bed and have a happy time? Why is the whole thing so tangled up with bloody concepts like honor?" (108). Judith has revealed herself to be less than ideal, and the discussion is surprising because of it. Perhaps because the cemetery has moved her to considerations of "time's wingèd chariot," she is far more willing (at least in theory) to commit adultery than is Tim. In fact, it seems as if all Tim has to do is ask. This is a reversal of the traditional man-the-hunter and woman-the-prey roles, and the remark that ends the scene turns his reservations into an adherence to the code of honorable behavior by which men ideally relate to one another: Tim says he could not have returned to "Gordon's smiling unsuspicious face" (108). Tim has held to that code when even Lancelot du Lac and Tristan did not—not that it is easy for him. His office relationship with Gordon continues "unruffled and secure," but, loving Judith was both pleasure and pain, delight and deprivation, wishes withdrawn, dreams denied" (135).

Near the end of *Banker,* after the mystery has been solved, Gordon is preparing to tour Asia and Australia. Tim will not see Judith for months. While Gordon is in the hospital for a checkup, Tim takes her to dinner. They tell "each other much without saying a word" (297). When he drives her home, they park in front and kiss lengthily, "floating in passion, dreaming in deep unaccustomed touch" (298). Eventually they draw back and hold hands:

> A long time passed.
> "We can't," I said eventually.
> "No."
> "Especially not," I said, "in his own house."
> "No." (298–99)

Just as at the previous opportunity, Tim is the one who speaks against the obvious, though this time Judith does not resist. It is still a question of a man's honorable relationship with other men. After all, it might be objected, it is certainly as much Judith's house as Gordon's, and Tim does not say that he and she should not violate *their* house.

The novel does not end here, though it seems like a good spot for closure. There is a good scene in which he flies a kite with Pen Warner, who has become friend and confidant. She tells him that Gordon trusts him, though he knows about Tim's love for his wife, and she urges Tim to "let Judith go" for his own sake. He reflects on all he has learned about grief, pain, and death but concludes he cannot begin searching for another woman. This scene is also a good spot for closing, but then Gordon has a convenient cerebral hemorrhage, which frees Judith for Tim. The ruptured vessel is a deus ex machina of the worst sort; it is one page too much of an excellent book. Such things do happen, and, of course, Tim does not wish to get Judith at Gordon's expense, but the ending is clearly contrived to be happy, and it is annoying, especially after the crisp, open ending of *Flying Finish*. Perhaps Tim deserves it after having gained such wisdom about the problems of life and the ironies of fate, but when fate turns so cooperative, it seems Francis has tried to undo in one page what he has so carefully stated about the fragile relationships between men and women and the often exacerbating necessity of honor. Call it a tactical error in an otherwise strategically successful novel.

Secondary Female Characters

Secondary female characters in Francis seem generally to fall into two general categories. The first is a frumpish older woman who has an almost military sense of self-control and discipline. Capable and reliable, she is usually harmlessly unsexy—the kind of woman who props her feet up, shares a good stiff drink with the hero, and has the experience to give him wise advice. She is not usually a warm person, though there is usually much affection between her, the hero, and the people who see inside her stony exterior. She has been through enough that she is tough, and she seems to believe that people need to work their way through their own problems. She will help but not interfere. Often she is a horse trainer. Imagining Sophie Randolph a few decades older and unattached creates an image of this type of character. Examples include Popsy in *The Danger*, who helps Alessia overcome her fears and get back into racing; Etty Craig, the Griffons' head lad in *Bonecrack*; and Margaret, the Griffons' secretary. Annie Villars of *Rat Race* also comes to mind, as well as Ursula Young of *Banker*, Antonia Hunterscombe of *Knockdown*, Lavinia Nore of *Reflex*, and the formidable Nerissa of *Smokescreen*. Pen Warner (*Banker*) is not as old as most of them but is similar in many other respects. The type is also recognizable in *Proof* with Flora and in both *Bolt* and *Break In* with the Princess. Each woman has distinctive characteristics, but like sisters, they are recognizably related.

Also recurring, though less frequently, is the adolescent woman verging on adulthood, lovable in her awkwardness, adamantly loyal to horses, a kind of little sister to the hero. The affection between the hero and this young woman is usually very deep. When Ginnie (*Banker*) becomes one of Francis's few women murder victims, Tim sobs in "tearing body-shaking grief" and speaks of how much he loved her, "as a friend; as a brother" (210). One of the "little people" in racing whom James Tyrone interviews is Sandy Willis, another example: "She loved her work, she loved Zig Zag [a horse in her care], the racing world was the tops, and no, she wasn't in any hurry to get married, there were always boys around if she wanted them and honestly whoever would swop Zig Zag for a load of draggy housework."[10] There is an interesting meeting of both this type of woman and the older type in *Bonecrack*'s Etty Craig who is described as having been much this type when she entered ladship as a nineteen year old, though she was not, apparently as ebullient as Ginnie and Sandy: "She seemed to like males well enough, but she treated them as she did her horses, with brisk friendliness, immense understanding, and cool unsentimentality" (25). There is an implicit sexuality in these young women, which becomes a problem only for the hero of *Blood Sport*. Lynnie has just turned seventeen and is described by narrator Gene Hawkins as having "a curvy figure, delicate neck, baby skin," but like other Francis heroes, Hawkins does not take advantage of "the notice-me flags of the pretty young female. . . . If I had learnt anything in thirty-eight years it was who not to go to bed with."[11] Lynnie even kisses him later, and not with friendly intentions, but Gene resists (154). Eunice Teller is quite astonished that Gene has not even tried to sleep with the nubile girl (139) and would be more astonished if she knew Lynnie had virtually offered, but that is because she misunderstands not only honor but the kind of relationship Gene and, by inference, the other Francis heroes have with these adolescent women. The book ends with Lynnie still infatuated with Gene and hoping to see him more, though he makes the possibility doubtful.

Francis is always doing themes and variations, however. A reader recognizes a familiar melody line taking a surprising turn. One of these is in the character of Hilary Pinlock, a frumpy headmistress who helps

Roland Britten hide from his kidnappers in *Risk*. She takes charge
immediately. Cool and collected, she curtly tells Roland what to do
and then conceals him in her hotel room. "It was as easy to stop Miss
Pinlock as an avalanche," remarks Roland (53). So far she is not much
different from Popsy and the other tough, mature women, but then
the surprise comes. "Will you go to bed with me?" she asks (55).
Roland is so astonished that she is embarrassed. The reason Pinlock is
vacationing alone in Minorca is that she has never had sex. Out of
"curiosity, and the pursuit of knowledge" (56) she has determined to
eliminate this problem. It will also, she thinks, make her a better
headmistress, particularly when dealing with her brash, modern students.
She has refused, however, to throw herself at an accommodating ski
instructor or waiter; it would not do to lose her dignity. She wants
"knowledge without guilt or shame." "The dream of Eden," comments
Roland (57). Despite the calculated motives and her being not sexually
attractive to Roland, he accommodates her to an unlikely level of
extreme pleasure. "It was the strangest love-making," says Roland, "but
it did work" (60). Later she helps him do some investigating, and he
gives her a present of a "long bold scarlet coat." It changes her from
"duck into swan," "a plain woman transfigured" (141). Plainly the
generous gift he has given her has changed her entire outlook on life.
Her sense of having missed something is gone, and she is freer, more
alive. It is another salvation by love, though the love here is more
charity than romance.

Blood Sport also has the hero saving a minor woman character. Eunice
Teller is a heavy-drinking wealthy housewife out of the Chandler tradition
(reminiscent of the Barbara Stanwyck role in the Chandler screenplay
Double Indemnity). "I have . . . bloody . . . everything," she says
miserably (73). She throws herself persistently at Gene Hawkins. She
is very much a suspect in the novel from the first time she tries to
seduce him by the pool, encouraging him to drink up and to "strip
off and get into the pool" (64). He eventually changes into a swimsuit,
and she plays a game of pointing his own gun at him. He concludes
she is "a very troubled lady" (68), and the thrust and parry continues
for several more pages. As he commented about Lynnie, however, Gene
knows who not to sleep with. Later he finds Eunice in his bed and
states flatly that he does not sleep with the wives or daughters of the
men he works for. She recognizes that he will not break this code and
says "explosively," "with an undoubted depth of unbearable truth,"
"I'm bored" (139). Like Andrew Douglas and many another Francis

hero, Gene clearly sees through to the problem and paternally explains that casual sex "can be a running away from real effort. A lover may be a sublimation of a deeper need. People who can't face the demands of one may opt for passing the time with the other" (141). A more pessimistic writer might face up to the fact that Eunice's kind of unhappiness does not go away with a little kindness, but Francis not only has the sodden floozy psychoanalyzed by Gene, the hero saves her. He suggests she turn her interest (and second sublimation), decorating, into a business. By the end of the novel, she is happily searching for business locations, fabrics, and objets d'art to redo other people's homes. The cure is sudden and remarkably successful considering Gene's inability to get rid of his own suicidal tendencies. The "curing" of Zanna Martin by Sid Halley in *Odds Against* is perhaps more plausible because it is mutual, but it is also not shown to have been easy.

David Cleveland is enticed by a married woman, Kari Kristiansen, in *Slayride*. She is much less direct than Eunice, and her unhappiness is not something David can do anything about. Arne, her husband, asks David, "Isn't she beautiful?" and David thinks, "Normally I disliked men who invited admiration of their wives as if they were properties like cars."[12] Arne also speaks of her "proprietorially" (25). At first, David thinks they are happy. He describes Kari as "a highly feminine lady with apparently no banners to wave about equality in the kitchen. . . . The proposition that everything indoors was her domain, and everything outside his seemed only to lead to harmony. In my own sister, it had led to resentment, rows, and a broken marriage. Kari, it seemed to me, expected less, settled for less, and achieved more" (64). David finds himself attracted to her but tells himself that an investigator like her husband will read their eyes, so he leaves.

Later David invites them to dinner at a hotel and discovers that the Kristiansen marriage is less than ideal. Nowhere near as blatant as Eunice, Kari nonetheless succeeds—in an extraordinary way—where Eunice fails. David asks her out to the dance floor:

She smiled and moved forward until our bodies were touching at more points than not, and no woman ever did that unless she meant to. What we were engaged in from that moment on was an act of sex: upright, dancing, and fully clothed, but an act of sex nonetheless. . . . Head up, neck straight, she looked more withdrawn and absent-minded than passionately aroused. Then quite suddenly her whole body flushed with heat, and behind her eyes and right through her very deeply I was for almost twenty seconds aware of a gentle intense throbbing. (121)

This strange public infidelity sourly turns off David. He thinks of Kari as a tease who has taken her own satisfaction and left him with nothing: "a selfish little pig." When he goes to bed that night, he hardly thinks about her at all (122). That is about all for Kari Kristiansen. The rest of the novel mentions her rarely, and the romantic attention shifts to David's friendly soothing of the widow of the jockey whose murder David is investigating. After a calm, domestic visit with the widow, complete with a hot scone from the oven, he plainly says he will be returning (155). That Kari is also a widow by the end of the book is inconsequential. Her sexual attractiveness is tarnished by her willingness to betray the marriage contract without resisting, even if only mentally. The woman or man without the ideal of self-control, Francis implies, can never be trusted.

Finally, as women are rarely the physical victims of crime in Francis, they are also rarely among the villains. Usually a bad woman is pathetic, like Eunice, or misguided, like Aunt Beatrice in *Bolt*. They may acquiesce to criminality, but their role is not as the demonic mastermind. They may be vain and unpleasant, they may be indifferent to normal family feelings, like Alessia's sister, but the conflict is usually man-to-man, with the women in roles little different from the weak-willed petty criminals who carry out the villain's orders. Doria Kraye is incredibly cruel in *Odds Against*. Egged on by her husband, she is about the nastiest female in all of the novels, but she is the exception. Grace Roxford has to be sat on by three strong men to hold her down after her knife attack in *Enquiry*, but she is pathetically demented and not responsible for her actions. The femme fatale devil-woman is not a congenial motif for Francis, yet another sign of a charmingly chivalrous attitude.

Conclusion

While Francis has been praised for taking risks with his women characters, he carefully avoids a fully pro-feminist outlook.[13] He does not go as far as has sometimes been asserted. He allows women good jobs and insists that they take personal responsibility for their lives. On the other hand, he consistently shows women in situations in which they are dependent on the hero not just for physical safety but for psychological stability. This may be merely the circumstance of always having the knightly male hero. After all, in some of the novels, many of the men are dependent on the hero also. He makes the plans;

everyone else pitches in. As with the heroes, Francis's women are patterned but with an always interesting mixture of newness along with their predictability, which in many ways makes them seem more like ordinary people than many novelists' ingenious character creations. The trouble with many clichés is that they turn out to be true. A realistic novelist cannot avoid the fact that many people are born clichés.

Francis's attitude to women, however, is not notably different from his attitude to men. Most are weak. Most have been buffeted by life. Those with courage survive and grow, "endure and prevail" in the words of Barry Baushka.[14] Women are part of the same moral struggle that all of humanity is engaged in. In this way, Francis shows a respect for women that many other writers do not. At the same time, his apparent distaste for the cruelties inflicted on women in so much of the media shows that he still retains a gentleman's respect for women. He cannot be faulted for that. It is hard to justify beating up women characters in the name of equality, when it will serve only to stimulate whatever misogynist or sexually brutal tendencies exist in society and ultimately imply that women are not equal. The novels show him attempting to balance traditional mores against contemporary values, and the obligations of a person—to be loyal, to try to do right, to overcome dependency—are the same in Francis whether that person is male or female. In his admittedly male-centered novels, a man leads because of his individual personality, not some male birthright, and he is always aware of his duty to others. A good man never subjugates— as the villains always attempt to do. Men and women need each other as partners.

Chapter Five

Eden for Sale

The World of the Track

A steady reader of Francis learns not only about horses and their care and nurturing but about the qualities of horse and man as they are tested in a world that is not so much a special corner of creation or a self-contained universe but a world among worlds, an island connected to thousands of other islands by various surprising bridges. All of society gets connected in some way to the society of the track, and the action played out there serves as a microcosmic drama of moral conflict. This consistent view of horse racing as an aspect of the world through which most of the universal values—courage, honor, integrity, defiance of pain—can pass allows readers who are not particularly interested in racing to take interest in the struggles between and nuances of good and evil that take place there. Francis achieves this in the way that most important writers do: by playing out the universal against the concrete and specific reality of an intimately known world. A reader, without necessarily knowing or caring about Francis's personal history, gets a strong sense of the smells, feelings, and people who take part in the "racing game," learning details about the lip tattooing of horses in the United States or the difference between hurdle races and steeplechase races or the determinants of odds for British bookies. Yet the mysteries are never so totally based on the specific knowledge of horse racing that only aficionados could enjoy the books. As reviewer Judith Rascoe remarked, "you needn't know or care anything about racing to be his devoted reader."[1] Francis manages to strike the careful balance between the universal and the specific and while doing so maintains a precise, moral vision of how the individual elements relate to each other and to the whole.

Part of the delight in picking up another Francis novel is discovering what occupation he will relate to horse racing. Many of his novels naturally center on jockeys (*Dead Cert, Nerve, Enquiry, Break In*), but jockeys need something to ride, so horse trainers, breeders, farmers, bloodstock agents, and stable lads are featured in *Bonecrack, Trial Run, Knockdown,* and *For Kicks.* Highly valued jockeys travel continually from course to course, so *Rat Race* features a pilot who taxis them and horse owners around. *Flying Finish* features a company that transports the horses from country to country. Highly valued jockeys are also celebrities and may need protection from kidnapping *(The Danger).* Where there is betting, there is corruption, so there are Jockey Club investigators *(Slayride)* and detectives *(Odds Against* and *Whip Hand).* Photos of races and racing people are needed *(Reflex),* along with racing newspapers and their writers *(Forfeit).* The world of racing also expands to include occupations that might not be necessarily connected to horses. As other occupations are drawn into the world of racing, a naive narrator can discover along with the naive reader the details of racing that more knowledgeable heroes take for granted. When the horse becomes loved as an aesthetic object, paintings of it will be wanted *(In the Frame).* When people gather for racing, they will want drinks, and a wine merchant is needed *(Proof).* Successful horses require big money to purchase and feed, and Tim Ekaterin is called in *(Banker).* In *Twice Shy,* a man develops a computer betting system that falls into the hands of a physics teacher. Even a motion picture star *(Smokescreen),* an inventor of toys *(High Stakes),* and an ex-spy *(Blood Sport)* turn up. The racing world is inclusive. It opens up to embrace not only many aspects of human endeavor but is shown to be almost geographically unlimited; novels take place in Norway, Russia, South Africa, Australia, the United States, and Italy, as well as Great Britain.

The Francis depiction of horse racing is therefore a worldview in the sense that despite racing's exoticism for the noninitiate and its seeming difference from everyday life, it is essentially, morally no different from the rest of human life. People must encounter and struggle with fate in the form of evil and good. They must choose and act on their choices, frequently without being intellectually certain which is the right one, though they must make the effort. An examination of several of the novels cannot help but reveal the particulars of this conflict. Francis's books inevitably develop according to this moral view. Because they are usually regarded as "light reads" (that is, they are primarily for entertainment), they conform to the general trend of the traditional mystery, which is to provide a momentary illusion of certainty in a world that has challenged all of our most-cherished beliefs. In the twentieth century, the age of relativity and an unending profusion of products, it is comforting to escape into Sherlock Holmes's London with its limited number of tobaccos or into Sam Spade's San Francisco with its simpler (though not always simple) distinctions between the bad guys and the good. Francis's racing world holds similar comforts.

He has admitted in his interview with Diana Cooper-Clark that he has a rather straightforward intention in his theme of good versus evil: "In all my stories, I have a moral duty to civilization. I try to improve the life of the main characters or of the people I'm writing about. I do try to write with a moral scene running through."[2] When Cooper-Clark follows up by asking Francis whether he agrees with André Gide's statement that Dashiell Hammett was the best American writer because he "never corrupted his art with morality," Francis says, "I don't think I would agree." His opinion is consistent with his novels. It is plain who is good and who is evil, and it is a credit to his writing ability that usually the books do not seem too overtly simplistic. Various reviewers have criticized Francis's villains for not having complex personalities. The psychopathic villains are motivated almost always by greed and curiously unbothered by even the most rudimentary introspection. They become, therefore, not so much personalities as forces that must be opposed. They may be clever and difficult to defeat, but they are rather like tornadoes or typhoons—demonic and formidable but straightforward in their devastating motion.

Their opponents, when Francis draws them best, are complex, at base the best sort of men this world can offer yet by no means angels. There is a sense, therefore, that although good and evil are at struggle in the world, the situation is somewhat fluid, or situational. The battle becomes almost a man-against-nature struggle, and much of it is fought inside the protagonist. He must choose among possible options in a given context, and there is no infallible code of morality that dictates what must be done in every situation. The heroes frequently operate on the fringes of society, by overlooking lesser evils—jockeys throwing unimportant races, for example—or by not informing the police of all the facts because family might be hurt (*Dead Cert*) or because an old man might go through a stressful homicide trial that would serve no purpose (*Bolt*).

The individual is the repository of justice, not society itself, which may be either ineffective or corrupt, though more often the former. These existential flexibilities in Francis's concept of morality make the theme of good versus evil more tolerable to modern readers, who might be sentimental for some golden age when the villains twirled their mustaches and were hissed but who feel the contemporary world certainly has as many and perhaps worse villains who disguise themselves behind nicely polished teeth and high-flown rhetoric. Francis gives the comfort of a true moral universe, yet does not give it an easy presumption that would make it seem antiquated or unsophisticated.

Christmas "Kit" Fielding

Break In features one of Francis's psychologically least interesting main characters, Christmas "Kit" Fielding. Reviewers on the whole, however, called *Break In* "special" and expressed great delight that Francis was spending more fictional time on horseback with "the high spirits of a homecoming" after his wine merchant, kidnap specialist, physics teacher, and banker protagonists.[3] Kit's second appearance, in *Bolt,* utterly redeems him and produces one of Francis's best books, but he is hard to take in his first outing. As Kit's given name implies, he is too good to be true in *Break In* and lacks the dark dimension of characters like Sid Halley. This is not to say Kit does not have some interesting traits. Oversized for a flat-racing jockey, Kit has become an excellent steeplechaser. He is a twin, born with his sister, Holly, on the holiday of his name, and he shares a mild power of telepathy with her. Holly has married Bobby Allardeck, the youngest member of a family that has been feuding with the Fieldings for generations. Kit is virtually the only Fielding willing to forgive this treason, although his octogenarian grandfather shows a bit of forgiveness. Unfortunately the possibilities implied by telepathic twins seem to irritate Francis's taste for realism, so he does not exploit it for the plot, as might be expected, despite mystery readers' general antipathy to the supernatural.[4] It reminds one of Anton Chekhov's chestnut that a gun hanging over the fireplace in a drama must be fired. The reader expects such a visible, dramatic entity to be exploited, but the telepathy hangs over the fireplace throughout *Break In* and serves only for a cute ending and a trivial wisp of jealousy by Bobby. In *Bolt,* the telepathy is pretty much abandoned.

Kit is so faultless in *Break In* there is a temptation to make his name seem symbolic, if not allegorical, seriously damaging his credibility as a character. If "Christmas" is supposed to indicate that Kit was born to bring an end to the Fielding-Allardeck feud—in some sense to save humanity from Satan's power—it is a mercifully undeveloped symbolism, though the events might be tortured into that interpretation. The name also points up Kit's unconvincing goodness. While it may be true that there are people in the world as understanding, patient, clever, and talented, it is also true that they are very difficult to accept by us usually ordinary, frequently impatient, and often bad-tempered readers. Too much goodness in a character is implausible and often dull—partly why the romantics asserted that Satan was the hero of Milton's *Paradise Lost*. Characters should be battlegrounds for good and evil and all the obscure shades of light and dark. Sid Halley, Rob Finn, James Tyrone, and Philip Nore are—as are most of the rest of Francis's best heroes. In contrast, Kit Fielding will accept a beating at the hands of his brother-in-law simply because he has determined to resist his family brainwashing against the Allardecks. Afterward Bobby feels bad that the enmity manifested itself, but Kit asserts and continues to show that he does not resent Bobby's attack. He also forgives Bobby when his father, Maynard, persuades Bobby to point a gun at him with the momentary intention of murder. This is the understanding that passes good sense. If Bobby's hatred of the Fieldings is so deeply inculcated, it is also a wonder that Bobby never shows it toward Holly, his wife, an always available target, and also that it never occurs to Kit that Bobby's violence might be directed against his sister someday. Bobby's explanation that Holly is so passive that she does not seem like a Fielding⁵ is not enough, given the burned oatmeal and broken vases that inevitably disturb marriages and lead to so much familial violence in our society. Further, incredibly, Kit shows no resentment toward Lord Vaughnley for arranging his entrapment and torture and even shakes hands with him. Lord Vaughnley asks,

"What can I say? . . . What am I to say when I see you [Kit] on racecourses?"
"Good morning, Kit," I said.
. . . "Yes, but, . . . after what we did to you at the Guineas . . ."
I shrugged, "Fortunes of war . . . I don't resent it, if that's what you mean . . . Seek the battle, don't complain of the wounds."

What they did to Kit at the Guineas, only a few hours before this reconciliation, was repeatedly shock Kit into unconsciousness with an electrical stun gun. One is almost afraid the gun has caused brain damage if Kit is willing to forgive so quickly. This is stoicism beyond the pale of normal behavior.

Despite these problems, *Break In* exploits the typical Francis paradigm of good versus evil. It retains the almost Manichaean vision of what racing should be against the corruption with which people infect it. In many ways it reveals the Francis worldview most clearly because it is so blatant. The purity of Kit's character serves to express the best aspects of the racing experience, and his adventures seeking justice in the sordid world of yellow journalism underscore the clean glory of his riding. Usually, however, the races are not essential to resolving a Francis plot. In *Break In,* the racing scenes are typical—nearly irrelevant to the main story, serving as paeans to racing as a whole. Were it not for Francis's skill at making the sensations of riding in a competitive race so vivid, these scenes might seem merely to be for characterization, time passing, or tension building. Instead they become one of the pleasures of his novels, as well as the moral point marshaled against evil's counterpoint.

The novel begins with a race characteristic of Francis. Kit is to ride North Face, a temperamental horse owned by "a middle-aged princess of a dispossessed European monarchy." As Kit and the Princess watch North Face "stalk around the ring," he describes it as "herring-gutted, ugly, bad-tempered, moody." Kit continues: "He tolerated me when he felt like it, and I knew his every mean move. . . . At ten he was still an unpredictable rogue, and as clever a jumper as a cat. . . . Three times we had fallen together on landing, he, each time, getting unhurt to his feet and departing at speed with indestructible legs, indestructible courage, indestructible will to win. I loved him and I hated him and he was as usual starting favorite" (13–14). North Face is about as nasty a horse with which a jockey can deal, but it is impossible not to have some affection for him because he is a great competitor and because he is a horse. It is impossible to hate a horse totally. The horse is beautiful in Francis. The horse is innocent in a way adult humans cannot be. Each horse has a personality of its own, and a sensitive person can come to know it. Some horses are mean-spirited, some are imperiously proud, some have great courageous hearts, and others run their races with the indifference of a retired couple on a Sunday drive. The horse is a sort of quadruped child that might kill you by acting stupidly or out of panic but could not do a bad thing out of malice. One cannot hold a horse any more responsible than one holds an idiot or a juvenile responsible. As nasty as North Face may be, he has no evil in his soul, like Adam before the Fall, and like all other horses, petulant or sweet tempered, he is part of the uncorrupted center of racing, a contrast to sinful humanity. On the racetrack, remarks Kit, "the rogues had four legs and merely bit."[6] Men, however, torture, murder, and steal. The horse is the moral locus for which racing was created and is essential to the glory of the simple, yet profound, pleasure of watching horses run. The horse seeks no material reward. The horse is like an athlete praised in one of Pindar's odes, a beautiful expression of pure competition.

Francis's heroes always come to understand the essence of the race. They emulate the morality of the horse. "I'd do it [race] for nothing," says Kit, "but being paid is better" (*Bo,* 152). Henry Grey simply says, "I like it, it's fun" (*FF,* 85). Such remarks reflect Francis's own words: "The simple fact is that I like riding horses, and I like the speed and challenge of racing. I cannot explain why all jockeys . . . are willing to take pain, cold and disappointment in their stride. . . . Why do people climb mountains, or swim the Channel? . . . Because they can, they want to, and in some obscure way, they feel they must" (*SQ,* 104). When he describes the pleasure of racing at Aintree, Francis describes the far end of the course: "No one is about; there is only the wind, the flying turf, and the long fences. There everything is simple. The confident stride of a good horse, the soaring lift over the birch, and the safe landing, these are the whole of life" (*SQ,* 74).

Vanity and greed are the two major sins people can bring to the track, and these can blind them to the point of racing. Francis's heroes are not impractical; his breeders, trainers, and jockeys strive to make a living, but they never lose sight of the aesthetic dimension—the pure pleasure of racing. As Kit says when he contemplates retirement, "I wanted four more years, or five, at the game I had a passion for. I wanted to race for as long as my body was fit and uninjured and anyone would pay me" (*BI,* 61). In the prologue of *Whip Hand,* Sid Halley dreams of riding. "Winning was all," he says. "Winning was my function . . . What I was born for" (1). What does he get from winning? Adulation; but that is not the most important thing: "the cheering lifted me up on its wings, like a wave. But the winning was all; not the cheering." When Halley wakes, he can still feel "the ripple of muscle through two striving bodies, uniting in one" (1–2). Philip Nore comments (ironically—his mother was an addict) that "winning put you higher than heroin" (*Re,* 83). Winning is important but not because it leads to cheering or money. It is important because it tells a person he has done his best. It is important because it takes place in a kind of spiritual communion between jockey and horse, the latter of which is the ideal of pure competition, running not for gain but because it loves to, out of instinct. The rider becomes one with this instinct, and the instinct—good and pure—can be raised up into the rider's soul.

When Kit tries to deal with the cussed North Face, he always finds a battle of wills, and the race in *Break In* is no different. He cannot cajole North Face with sweet words and affection the way he can other horses, and even before the race begins, he calls it "a bastard, a sod, and a bloody pig." As they initially fall behind, the invective increases: "race, you bastard, race, or you'll end up as dogmeat, I'll personally kill you, you bastard . . . so get on with it, start racing, you sod, you bastard, you know you like it" (16). Notice that final remark; the horse is fighting its own instinct, and there is nothing to do but wait until the "demonic fit" burns itself out and North Face yields to his inborn urge to race. Before he does, however, he leaps the water jump in a way that would throw any jockey who is not familiar with him, and Kit swears to himself that he will "never ride the brute again." He adds, however, "Not ever. Never. I almost believed I meant it." Like exasperated parents who cannot ultimately bring themselves to disown their children, Kit cannot reject this being who becomes part of him when they race. North Face relents. "As if he'd been a naughty child who knew its tantrums had gone too far, he suddenly began to race. . . . North Face put back his ears and galloped with a flat, bloody-minded stride, accelerating toward the place he knew was his, that he'd so willfully rejected, that he wanted in his heart" (17). Despite the hopelessness of their position, they win, and once the race ends, the spiritual communion ends: "There was nothing coming from the horse's mind now: just a general sort of haze that in a human one would have interpreted as smugness. Most good horses knew when they had won; they filled their lungs and raised their heads with pride. Some were definitely depressed when they lost. Guilt they never felt, nor shame nor regret nor compassion: North Face would dump me the next time if he could" (18).

To emphasize that it is the race itself, the process, that is important, not the reward, Francis then describes Kit going through the awarding of the trophy. Kit has told the reader earlier that this race is heavier in prestige than prize money and that the *Sunday Towncrier,* the sponsor, is getting "maximum television coverage for minimum outlay" (15), thus deemphasizing the material reward of the race for him and revealing the intrusion of commercialism. Once the race ends, the prose turns quite matter of fact. The intensity of the race itself is lost. Kit is casual when the Princess tells him, "There's a trophy," and when he sees the ashamed jockey he beat out in the stretch, he remarks, "No one else paid much attention to his loss or to my win. The past was the past: the next race was what mattered" (19). Throughout the presentation, Kit is more interested in finding his sister and says he is grateful that the prize is not the usual cufflinks, as he already has more of them than he has shirts with French cuffs. Prizes mean little. He even deflects the praise directed to him by saying, "We were lucky" (20).

The races so dynamically and vividly portrayed in Francis usually have little bearing on the unraveling of the mysteries, and although the hero (if he is a jockey) is more often a winner than a loser, his winning usually is not crucial to the outcome. Admiral's fall in *Dead Cert* is, of course, the beginning of the mystery, and Alan York gets his revenge in the final race of the book, though the winner is never revealed. Rob Finn of *Nerve* must win in order to prove he has not lost his courage, but he undoes the villain in a way not connected to a particular race. In *Odds Against,* Sid Halley's nostalgic ride around the Seabury course leads to the discovery of a mirror intended to dazzle riders and cause an accident. In other novels, the races are even more peripheral to the protagonist's world. Yet the frequent descriptions of races in Francis's novels serve as more than just local color. They serve as the level of stasis that the criminality upsets, the level that the hero and plot inexorably move to restore. This resembles very much the classic form of comedy in which an ideal world is discombobulated in order to be later restored—for example, in Shakespeare's comedies in which "much ado" with love potions and disguises inevitably leads to most of the main characters' getting happily married to the proper partner.[7] In Francis, the Edenic world of racing is violated and disrupted by a crime that has widening implications, and the protagonist's task is to put matters right.

The Disrupted World

In *Break In,* the pattern of stasis, disruption, and restoration works in the following manner. Bobby and Holly are making a passable living training horses. Like most other people starting a business, they are living on a margin of credit. The goodwill of their creditors is essential; money does not come in steadily but by seasons. They are not wealthy but are happy. Holly is pregnant, the creditors are content, and everything is in equilibrium. The serpent enters Eden in the form of yellow journalism from the *Daily Flag*'s "Intimate Details" page: "Folks say the skids are under Robertson (Bobby) Allardeck (32), race horse trainer son of tycoon Maynard Allardeck (50). Never his father's favorite (they are not talking), Bobby has bought more than he can pay for, and guess who won't be coming to the rescue. Watch this space for more" (21–22). This sleazy bit of gossip causes immediate instability. The creditors get nervous. If Bobby's business fails, the feed men, blacksmith, veterinarians, and other suppliers will lose all they have advanced to him in the normal course of business. Bobby cannot obtain normal supplies and services until he pays all his previous debts and pays all future ones up front. Bobby and Holly will lose everything.

Francis often begins his novels with a crime that is not immediately obvious as a crime. The newspaper has been nasty but not blatantly criminal. A body has not tumbled out of the closet. An apparently small evil infects the body of horse racing and spreads to become a raging fever. Often it is only the hero who recognizes the seriousness of the initial event. *Blood Sport,* for example, begins with a boating accident that only the hero recognizes was actually attempted murder. *Banker* begins with a man having a peculiar—almost humorous— reaction to his medication. *Proof* hints of future trouble when a man notices that his Laphroig whisky is not Laphroig, followed by a peculiar accident when a vehicle rolls into a tent of crowded people. Philip Nore of *Reflex* takes a normal fall from a horse, is approached by a solicitor who wants him to visit his estranged grandmother, and then finds himself instructed to lose a race—the last being a small evil, which the reader comes to recognize is not unusual though it is offensive. *Nerve* begins with a messy suicide, but it does not seem to be anything other than an individual act of despair. *Forfeit* starts with a drunk reporter falling to his death, and *Flying Finish* has two men abandoning their jobs and running off for no known reason. *Bolt* has Kit Fielding stumble into a confrontation that escalates from a disagreement to total war in subsequent chapters. Francis never begins a book slowly, even when he takes up this strategy in which evil's rape begins as an ambiguous leer, and several of his novels begin with the hero in definite, though often seemingly motiveless, criminal pincers. Examples include *Risk* and *Bonecrack,* in which the hero is being assaulted, and *In the Frame* when Charles Todd's cousin's wife has been murdered because she stumbled into a burglary. With these possible exceptions, however, the first shock of evil in a Francis novel is usually mild, an unfortunate accident or peculiar incident.

The voltage always increases, however, as it does in *Break In,* and subsequently more serious attacks follow. When Kit approaches Lord Vaughnley, the owner of a newspaper rival to the *Flag,* in an attempt to discover who is trying to ruin Bobby, the following words are exchanged:

"Hm," Lord Vaughnley said. "Too bad. But, my dear fellow, pointless attacks are what the public likes to read. Destructive criticism sells papers, back-patting doesn't. My father used to say that, and he was seldom wrong."
"And to hell with justice," I said.
"We live in an unkind world. Always have, always will. Christians to the lions, roll up, buy the best seats in the shade, gory spectacle guaranteed. People buy newspapers, my dear fellow, to see victims torn limb from limb. Be thankful it's physically bloodless, we've advanced at least that far." He smiled as if talking to a child. (27).

There are several revelations in this conversation, not the least of which is that Kit is a bit of a child in his purehearted quest for justice—something a reader could not say about Francis's better-drawn characters. Further the idealization of the horse and its motivations (or Kit's understanding of them) can now be contrasted with the corruptibility and insipient venality of humanity. Humans have free will and therefore have the potential to go bad. It begins small. People are amused by hearing nasty comments about distant people; gossip becomes an addictive entertainment. It becomes impossible for a newspaper with a sense of justice to survive. Little nastinesses become commonplace, and we should be thankful they are not worse; usually only feelings get hurt. What perpetuates and encourages these evils? Money. Vaughnley says it "sells" paper and in his second comment uses the word *buy* twice. The love of money is the root of all evil, or at least the greater part of it in Francis's novels.

The hero is a typical hard-boiled hero in being incorruptible when it comes to money. It is Kit who is concerned with justice and is generous with his own money in bailing out Bobby and Holly. The hero is also not prey to the other primary sin of Francis's villains: vanity and its partner, envy. Typically Kit envies no one, even those people who have not been orphaned. The villains, on the other hand, are greedy, prideful, tyrannical, and consumed by envy. They are not usually very complex, committing murder, for example, out of love, loyalty, patriotism, or some other potentially justifiable motive. Possible exceptions might include Enso Rivera of *Bonecrack,* who is madly acting out of misguided love for his son, and Maurice Kemp-Lore of *Nerve* who has been mentally disturbed by his own failure. Neither sympathy for the devil nor the ironies of good darkening into evil seem to appeal to Francis. His heroes may have money or not have money, but they are untainted by it. They may be obviously successful or marginally successful, but they are not self-important. The opposite is true of his villains. David Cleveland sums it up for almost all Francis malefactors when he explains the villain's behavior to his son: "They [all these things] happened because your father is both greedy and proud, which is always a pretty deadly combination" (*Sl,* 202).

Francis has remarked that one of the reasons he does not write about professional detectives is that there is too much of the criminal mind in them (paralleling Freud's often-quoted observation that a man becomes a policeman because he senses his own predisposition to crime). Francis has admitted that he identifies so closely with his main character that it is impossible to put criminal leanings in him. "I haven't got any criminal leanings at all, I don't think," he has said.[8] His villains are therefore exaggerated, less human than demonic, for to be human in Francis is to have weaknesses but also, when uncorrupted by civilization, to have at core a Rousseau-like goodness.

Maynard Allardeck

Bobby Allardeck's father is a typical Francis villain in many ways and the only villain to survive into a second novel. Maynard is the central star in a constellation of bad guys in both *Break In* and *Bolt.* He is rotten to the core and inspires much of the evil that he himself does not create. Maynard's evils begin with the total metastasis of the Fielding-Allardeck feud through him. Kit explains that there had been a "bitter mutual persisting hatred" between the families "further back than anyone could remember." When Charles II held court in New-market, a Fielding and an Allardeck were knifing each other. Another Allardeck likely robbed and killed a Fielding over a bet at Queen Anne's race course. A dual in the Regency period resulted in one dead from each family. In the Victorian period, charges of cowardice and seduction (both true) led to a fight that nearly killed an Allardeck. There were a barn burning and shotgun confrontations later and an ongoing cycle of vicious competition in the racing business: "if coming first and second in the same race [they] lodged objections against each other as a matter of course" (*BI*, 44–46).

In Kit's lifetime, however, several things have combined to soften the enmity. Kit and Holly's father died, and Maynard Allardeck left racing for other—as it turns out, shady—businesses. The Fielding grandfather suspects Allardecks constantly, but when Holly plays Juliet to Bobby's Romeo and unites the warring families, the old man, angered as he is, gradually comes to a grudging acceptance and does not totally reject her. Kit and Bobby have become friendly enough, says Kit, that if they each had children, the new generation could be friends. Kit resists the impulse to prejudice, and it seems a little too easy, especially when he is attacked by Bobby, when Bobby nearly kills him at Maynard's urging, and when he discovers how thoroughly vile Maynard is. Gradually the disease of the feud, however, is diminishing among all the parties with the exception of Maynard. Maynard has rejected his son because he married a Fielding. He hates Kit because he is a Fielding. He says to Kit at one point, "You're filth by birth, you're not worth the fuss that's made of you, and I'd be glad to see you dead" (*BI*, 81–82). That sums up his attitude but not his evil.

Even Kit's grandfather, whose chief regret at eighty-two is that he does not have Maynard's father with whom to match spiteful wits, finds Maynard a special case of the bad seed, not just a "power-hungry egomaniac" but also a "creeper": "A bully to the weak but a bootlicker to the strong." When he was young, he told old Fielding that he was going to grow up to be a lord because then Fieldings would have to bow to him (*BI*, 59). On top of Maynard's nursing the feud, therefore, he is also filled with an enormous vanity, which holds central importance in unraveling why someone has started a smear campaign against Bobby. Maynard is working hard to get himself knighted. Unlike Kit, whose goal in riding is the process of racing, Maynard's goal in his life is the acquisition of the reward. Vanity in Francis's novels usually travels hand in glove with greed, and here it is inseparable from Maynard's egomania.

Gradually the reader discovers that Maynard has made his wealth by unethical company take-overs, similar to (but more refined than) the way Ganser Mays takes over betting shops in *High Stakes*. His modus operandi is to approach an overextended business with loans on easy terms. The business sees him as its savior and accepts his offer. As soon as the business has recovered, Maynard gently asks for repayment. To pay would force the business to close, with all its attendant layoffs and other hardships. Maynard, "the humanitarian," therefore agrees to accept the business itself in lieu of payment, and the employees (except for owners and directors) thereby retain their jobs. Quickly, then, Maynard sells his revitalized company to a larger conglomerate for a hefty profit (*BI,* 26). Maynard calls it "classic take-over procedure"; the maneuver is totally legal. The fact that it is, just like the rumor-mongering of the yellow press, is another of Francis's implications that the law is not the full reservoir of justice, especially when it is apparent that Maynard ironically expects to earn a knighthood for his "services to industry."

Legality does not mean that people will not unjustly suffer. Two quintessentially British elder characters, Major C. Perryside and his wife, Lucy, have their only joy (a horse named Metavane) stolen from them in the same way Maynard steals companies. He loaned them money; then, somehow, not so mysteriously, Metavane became lame, and Maynard called in his debt, accepting the horse in lieu of payment. The horse almost immediately recovered, and Maynard syndicated it. Then there is the story of George Tarker, whose despair turns to suicide by electrocution after Maynard loots his company. Human misery follows in the corrupt Maynard's wake, and the law is either too weak or society itself is too corrupted to deal with it. Francis in *Break In* approaches but does not embrace the Chandler vision of Los Angeles, a society gone bad, from top to bottom, in which only the victims (but not always the victims) can be innocent.

In *Bolt,* Maynard's loathsomeness attains new levels. Francis has always been extraordinarily talented in evoking a sense of horror. The combination of his usually cool tone in describing pain and brutality and the cruel sadism of the murder techniques themselves can make even the most hardened readers grind their teeth. The gratuitous torture of Sid Halley in *Odds Against* springs immediately to mind, as well as the actual bonecracking in *Bonecrack.* In *Flying Finish,* when the sadistic Billy shoots bloody lines across Henry Grey's chest, carefully making certain the bullet does not penetrate a rib but merely scrapes the flesh off, the reader is shaken. *Proof* offers even more horror. When the first murder victim is discovered, Tony Beach describes him: "He was dead. He had to be dead. For head, above the bare stretched neck, he had a large white featureless globe like a giant puffball, and it was only when one fought down nausea and looked closely that one could see from the throat up he had been entirely, smoothly and thickly encased in plaster of paris."[9] Readers will not easily forget the shock of learning that a man might be murdered by encasing his head in a cast. Long after plot, title, and characters are vague, this will be remembered with a shudder. Readers can have no doubt of the evil of someone who could do this to a human being, regardless of how much the victim may have been criminally involved.

A writer can increase the horror of such sadism if the victim is a total innocent. With adult victims, there is usually a suspicion that the person may have brought it upon himself or herself or, at the very least, could not have reached adulthood without a tinge of sin. Child killing is so distasteful that it is relatively rare in literature, though there are notable exceptions, as in Shakespeare's *Richard III*. Francis rattles the reader of *The Danger* with a description of how the kidnappers intended to rid themselves of three-year-old Dominic by dropping him down a chute into a bricked-up chamber (250) and with his realistic description of the child after he is rescued (255–65). Dominic is convincingly described, and Francis has not the heart to do him bodily harm.

A horse, too, is like a child. It is innocent, and it is dependent on human beings for its sustenance. A three-year-old horse may be a professional runner, but in all other respects it is a three-year-old that will never mature. The death of any horse is a melancholy object, even when necessary. In *Flying Finish* Henry Grey kills a maddened horse, Okinawa, who might cause the plane in which it is being transported to crash. Grey is portrayed as an emotionally cold man, and he describes slashing Okinawa's carotid artery in unemotional language: "I don't know how many pints of blood there should be in a horse; the colt bled to death and his heart pumped out nearly every drop. My clothes were soaked in it, and the sweet smell made me feel sick. I stumbled down the plane into the lavatory compartment and stripped to the skin, and washed myself with hands I found to be helplessly trembling" (62). Notice that he "found" his hands to be trembling. The emotion of this necessary killing startles Grey and haunts him later. The effect on less reserved people is even stronger. In *Bolt,* the mechanics of the humane killer (bolt) must be explained to Kit, which surprises the veterinarian. Over time, a jockey rides a number of mounts who break their legs, but Kit has always left before the killing: "One moment you're in partnership with that big creature, and maybe you like him, and the next moment he's going to die. . . . It may be odd to you . . . but I have never seen the gun actually put to the head" (84). While this serves to reveal how a bolt works, it also serves to define Kit's character and the ideal relationship between jockey and beast.

Francis's villains, however, are outside the chain of human sympathy. As Bill Graham, a real-life detective who spends his life investigating insurance claims on the death of horses, told an interviewer: "A man who'll kill a horse is a diabolical bastard."[10] To kill a horse out of greed is certainly diabolical and would disgust any decent person; to kill horses in order to punish their owners or riders takes evil to its quintessence. When Kit is told that two of his mounts have been killed, he reveals the equivalency by immediately turning them human: "Cascade and Cotopaxi . . . people I knew, had known for years. I grieved for them as for friends" (*Bo*, 78). Although the law cannot extend protection to horses as it does to people, certainly the emotional response is that such killings are the equivalent of murder. This makes Francis's villains who do so exaggeratedly demonic. In *Bonecrack*, Enso Rivera's breaking horses' legs inevitably results in their being put down, and it is made plain by the end of the novel that he is probably suffering from insanity caused by terminal syphilis. In *Banker*, the tormenting of horses by various medicinal tricks accentuates the evil, and the nobbling of horses using torture, a dog whistle, and the Pavlovian reaction is nearly unbearable in *For Kicks*. In *Bolt*, the use of a humane killer to destroy promising mounts makes both Henri Nanterre and Maynard Allardeck into fiends.

Many of Francis's villains are intent on breaking the will of their victims. They want not just to have their way but to make others subservient to them. Almost like Big Brother in *1984*, they want people not just to acquiesce but to love them. Sometimes this is more important to the villain's vanity than simply defeating the opponents and can be observed in *Bonecrack, Forfeit,* and *Whip Hand*, among others. Freedom is the right of all human beings in Francis, and the attempt to restrain that freedom is one of the worst evils. The impulse to resist coercion is one of the qualities that drag the heroes into trouble. Jonah Dereham will not be bullied into going along with bloodstock schemes. Philip Nore develops the impulse to resist throwing races. Randall Drew of *Trial Run* will not stop investigating almost because there are threats to do so. Daniel Roke seeks a life outside his obligations and then faces the horror of accepting submission in order to maintain his cover. Henry Grey chafes at the shackles of his noble birthright. Kelly Hughes fights back when one of the greatest experiences of freedom, riding, is unjustly denied him.

In a more physical sense, Francis heroes are often subject to claustrophobic imprisonment or torture. The confinements Roland Britten suffers in *Risk* are extraordinarily airless and vivid. Edward Link is handcuffed in a car, Alan York is assaulted in the confines of a horse trailer, and Andrew Douglas, after helping kidnap victims overcome their nightmares of imprisonment, finds himself chained to a tree. Rob Finn is hung from a chain in a barn and eventually evens the score by confining his allergy-plagued adversary with a horse. The most extreme claustrophobic horror in all of Francis, however, is undoubtedly *Proof*'s murder by encasement in plaster.

Freedom is also a responsibility in Francis. Humans are free to choose, but they must live with the consequences of choice. As in Camus and Sartre, they are "condemned to freedom." There is no way ultimately to escape making choices. Philip Nore learns this as the novel *Reflex* develops and is the most refined example of the protagonist moving from wishing his "condemnation" away to embracing it. When Francis heroes are tolerant of petty criminals, there is often an attitude that it is a pity people fall back on their weaknesses instead of seeking freedom, but that is only their problem until they begin to impose on other people's choices. The pathetic Bert Checkov of *Forfeit* warns James Tyrone against selling his column, as he has done, and Tyrone refuses, despite all the suffering it might cause, to submit to the criminal Vjoesterod's control. Jonah Dereham's attitude toward his brother's alcoholism is that Crispin himself must choose to cease drinking; Jonah does little about it. The Francis hero rarely puts himself in the position of restraining anyone else's freedoms and is sympathetic if someone chooses badly because he or she has wasted the possibilities.

Henri Nanterre of *Bolt* follows the pattern of freedom-crushing villains by attempting to coerce Roland de Brescou, invalid husband of the princess who hires Kit as her jockey, to sign documents making it possible for Nanterre to manufacture a plastic pistol that terrorists, for example, would find easy to smuggle aboard airplanes. Loosing yet another potential source of evil upon the world is of no concern to the oily Frenchman Nanterre. There are tremendous profits to be made, and he is psychopathic enough to use whatever threats and cruelties he can to force de Brescou to sign. All that stands between him and millions of francs is the stubborn pride of a wheelchair-ridden aristocrat who regards the sale of weapons as a blot on the escutcheon. It is not long after Nanterre's initial threats that two horses capable of winning the Grand National are shot with a bolt. Nanterre rants, raves, and threatens on the telephone and in person. He bribes the foolish Aunt Beatrice (de Brescou's sister) to spy on her own family. He ambushes

Danielle de Brescou (the daughter and Kit's love) when she gets off work by flattening two of her tires. He arranges to have Prince Litsi, an ally of Kit, pushed off a grandstand. Later he is caught planting a bomb in Kit's car, and Kit ties him to it. By this point, part of the reader wishes that Kit would simply use his remote car starter and efface this revolting bully from the earth. Kit does not, of course, but it is not just what the reader has seen that makes Nanterre so horrible. Earlier a trainer, Mrs. Roqueville, tells Kit with disgust how Nanterre claimed he was afraid the knackers would patch up a filly of his that contracted navicular and make a profit at his expense. "The filly was put down . . . ," she says, "with Nanterre watching" (144). The implication is clear. Nanterre enjoys seeing the horse die. The contrast with Kit is obvious.

The Frenchman is not the only villain in *Bolt,* however. Maynard Allardeck, even more repulsive than he was in *Break In,* hovers throughout the novel, still nursing his irrational hatred of Kit, pumped up by Kit's having prevented his knighthood. As in *Break In,* Maynard is a kind of evil star at the center of an evil constellation. He uses his position as steward to torment Kit whenever possible, and he is nonetheless held in respect at the track. His superficial manners conceal the rottenness of his soul—if he has one. As the wife of a trainer observes in discussing Nanterre, "I expect the Marquis de Sade was perfectly charming on the racecourse. . . . It is where anyone can pretend to be a gentleman" (144). Kit does little to expose him, however. Early in the novel, Kit, because of his fear that he is losing Danielle to the charming Prince Litsi, presses his mount, Cascade, too hard in winning a race, to the point he is afraid the horse might drop dead from an overstrained heart. He is ashamed and takes "little joy in the victory" (14). Human troubles should not be turned on the innocent. Oddly, perhaps, after Kit's saintliness in *Break In,* this initial situation helps establish him as a much more credible character, and it is one of the reasons *Bolt* is a much more successful novel. Kit has a small cut on his soul for punishing the horse, and he is trying to face up to his guilt when he sees Maynard, as steward, checking Cascade for signs of being overworked.

Maynard, of course, is only using Cascade to get back at Kit. Feigning care for the horse, he examines it for weals, but ironically, the horses were too bunched for Kit to use the whip he raised and harshly would have brought down. Kit muses there might be "whip marks on Cascade's soul" but not on his hide, and Maynard is frustrated once again.

Maynard reappears throughout the novel, evilly glowering at Kit, implying he has ridden poorly, all the while maintaining his lordly manners to everyone else. Later, when the news about Kit's hold over Maynard (the videotape from *Break In*) leaks out, Maynard finds an opportunity to shove Kit down a staircase. Kit is almost relieved that Maynard's "murderous" nature can be vented with these little cruelties. Unfortunately, however, these small evils Maynard is perpetrating only conceal the far greater evils, which are dramatically revealed in the stunning final chapter. When Maynard is ironically killed with a bolt by a furious trainer, the clear implication is that a mad dog has been put out of his misery. The elderly trainer is coached by Kit to avoid the legal ramifications of having "put down" Maynard, and Francis gives us another instance of justice being achieved by operating outside the law, just as Kit has done with Henri Nanterre. The niceties of the law are not overly important when confronting pure evil.

The Power of the Press

Maynard is the central star in a constellation of evil. In *Break In* those who have been victimized by Maynard set upon revenge but, being corrupted themselves, think nothing of destroying the innocent in their attempt to get even. It is gradually revealed that the innuendo and lies that have appeared in the paper are a backhand way of getting at Maynard. As in *Bolt,* much of the wrongdoing that happens in *Break In* is not Maynard's. Lord Vaughnley, along with Nestor Pollgate, is capable of hiring thugs and torturing Kit. Vaughnley, owning the *Towncrier,* and Pollgate, owning the *Flag,* have been unethical and criminal in their attempt to deny Maynard the knighthood he has wanted since childhood. This is but one example of the recurrent criticism Francis had directed at the press. Snide gossip columns are frequently quoted in his novels as examples of corruption. Insensitive to human feeling and justice, the yellow press is consistently shown to be one of the worst elements involved in racing, contaminated by its need to sell papers.

This slant on the press is interesting because Francis first wrote as a newspaperman. John C. Carr asked Francis how he liked being a journalist. Francis replied, "I got used to it. . . . I can't say I really liked it because I hated—If you picked up a little bit of news that wasn't quite proper and if you could use it, editors, quite rightly so, expected you to use it, but I hated to print anything in the paper that would give the people I was writing about a black name, a dirty name."[11] Earlier, while saying the press had done racing "a lot of good," he had warmed up to this confession by saying, "The press only has to get a *hint* of something and they will blow it up and make mountains out of moleheaps." While not usually central to the plot, as in *Break In,* there are abundant examples throughout Francis's novels of distasteful journalism, usually in the form of direct quotations that simulate the style of such writing. One is reminded of John Hawkes's excellent simulations in the name of Sydney Slyter in his literary novel *The Lime Twig,* a quasi-mystery set in the world of British horse racing.

James Tyrone of *Forfeit* is a character whose feelings about his work for a sensational newspaper, the *Sunday Blaze,* are similar to Francis's own feelings about working for the press. In fact, there is a great deal about Tyrone that comes from Francis's personal experience, including the difficulties of dealing with a wife paralyzed by poliomyelitis. Mary Francis was struck down by the disease for a period, and it is obvious from the convincing anguish that Tyrone experiences in doing the elementary care for his wife, Elizabeth, that this is not a subject Francis has merely researched. A reader gets a strong sense of what it takes to bear up under the situation and, by implication, the character of a man who would not simply turn his wife over to a home. Tyrone indeed has misgivings about the effects of scandal mongering. Ironically, however, he is one of the best for "blowing the roof off." He regularly gets crank letters for his crusading articles, and his editor, Luke-John Morton, is always urging his writers to no-holds-barred articles that get the *Blaze* sold.

The moral ambiguities of Tyrone's situation indicate that Francis has a more subtle sense of the struggle between good and evil than his egregiously bad villains would seem to imply. Tyrone continually makes decisions about what he tells his editor in order to avoid involving innocent people, such as his girlfriend, Gail, and his wife. He knows the damage public scrutiny can do yet that some people deserve it. The *Blaze* can be a force for good or for harm, and it is important to him that he try to steer it when possible. The editor, Luke-John, is not so particular. If a story sells papers and will not drown them in the undertow of a libel suit, he prints it. Who gets hurt is not his concern. Tyrone, however, does the best he can under the circumstances to adhere to his personal code. If he did not work for the *Blaze,* he might have to leave his wife to the charity of the government. Which is the worse evil: abandoning his moral responsibility to his spouse or working in an often amoral, occasionally immoral, business? He has sold out in a sense, but not out of greed or vanity.

One of his adjustments to his situation consists of accepting a job as ghostwriter for ex-jockey Buster Figg's autobiography, and the similarity of names sounds like an allusion to Francis's getting talked into writing Lester Piggott's biography despite his initial refusal. Tyrone does not like the job and describes Buster as one of those successful people in the racing game who has lost touch with its purpose: "All he's interested in is the money. . . . He gambled in thousands. And he insists I put his biggest bets in" (2). Of course, all Tyrone is interested in is getting his money for ghosting, but again for Elizabeth's sake. He is also shown doing a magazine article for *Tally,* a background piece on the Lamplighter Gold Cup. The *Tally* editor evidently knows Tyrone can write without the "yellow" element as he pays Tyrone well and specifies he wants "the style and the insight but not the scandal" (5). Tyrone chooses to write about noncelebrities involved in the race: a couple who won a horse in a raffle, a second-class Irish jockey, and the groom of the best horse in the race. In doing so, Tyrone highlights the often forgotten people who make racing possible, who do it out of love for horses or for fun, and the article does much good. The Irish jockey gets his first important ride, for example, and he wins. No one is hurt by Tyrone's article—the subjects all benefit—though it is part of what draws Tyrone into his battle against the elegant, consummately evil South African Vjoersterod, a typical psychopathic, vain, and greedy Francis villain.

There are limits beyond which Tyrone will not go. The mystery begins when the drunk Bert Checkov falls from a window after warning Tyrone, "Don't sell your sodding soul. . . . Never sell your column" (10). Checkov has. Bought first and blackmailed after, he has succumbed to the attractions of the quick quid and now cannot escape. He knows Tyrone is always "bloody stony" broke because of Elizabeth and perhaps fears that Tyrone is corruptible, although in his drunkenness he says he knows Tyrone would not let it happen to him. Subsequent events prove Checkov right. Vjoersterod cannot force Tyrone into Checkov's situation. In order to prevent blackmail, Tyrone tells his wife about his affair with Gail. The price he pays is the knowledge that preserving his integrity has cost Elizabeth whatever peace of mind she had. He muses, "Don't sell your soul, Bert Checkov said. Don't sell your column. Sacrifice your wife's peace instead" (139). Later he thinks: "After all the shielding, which had improved her physical condition, I'd laid into her with a bulldozer. Selfishly. Just to save myself from a particularly odious form of tyranny. If she lost weight or fretted to breakdown point it would be directly my fault; and either or both seemed possible" (162). Even for Elizabeth, for whom he has sacrificed so much, there is a moral core that cannot be compromised. From the first attack on him, he tells her doctor, Antonio Perelli, that there are some situations he cannot walk away from, even for Elizabeth's sake (93). Life may be bloody, as Elizabeth says, but there are certain things a man has to do in order to remain a man. This is only partly Francis's message because he also shows that a man should not "sweat the small stuff." The distinction between what is small and what will corrupt the soul is left to each individual. Humans are left these existential choices, and the decision is usually not all that clear.

Particularly interesting is the moral accommodation Tyrone makes at the close of the novel. After having deliberately deceived his lover, Gail, into thinking that he cannot leave his wife because she is rich, Gail discovers the truth. Exactly why he has not told her from the beginning, or at the point at which he recognizes his deepening love for Gail, is also perplexing. It perhaps masochistically salves his conscience to let Gail think he is corrupted by his wife's money. It also helps keep a suitable distance between them so that the stickiness of a truly intimate relationship can be avoided. Her seeming liberality about sexual relations is one reason he is willing to let the affair begin. Also there is the obvious trait of Francis heroes: they despise being pitied. There seems to be no solution to Tyrone's situation other than a hellish cycle of sex with an accommodating stranger and inevitable regret. He will not leave Elizabeth, and his love for Gail practically requires him to leave her or become even more frustrated.

Yet there is a tentative solution. Elizabeth is responsible for it, mostly because Tyrone cannot bring himself to ask her to make further sacrifices and is not cruel or self-centered enough to insist on some relief. After a long talk with Dr. Perelli, she recognizes her husband's courage and loyalty; she understands that she gains nothing in seeking to take James's freedom away from him and takes a courageous step: "I was so afraid of losing you, I couldn't see how much I was asking of you. But I understand now that the more I can let you go, the easier you will find it to live with me . . . and the more you will want to" (246–7).

Is Francis advocating open marriage? Of course not. Life's bloody and people must try to do the best they can against such evils as gangsters and polio. The accommodation is not ideal. His double relationship with Gail and Elizabeth will likely lead to terrible stresses, both from the society around him and from within the ménage itself. Human beings, however, must seek to live. They must persevere against the violences with which life assaults them. Tyrone, Elizabeth, and perhaps Gail are doing the best they can in a severe situation, and hard-nosed morality provides no adequate solution. Evil is blatant, but much of coping with evil is not so clear. Who is to judge them? Who is to judge Tyrone for either of his accommodations: in his professional life or his personal? The adjustments to their marriage allowed by Elizabeth mirror the adjustments Tyrone has made in his life as a writer.

A number of novels similarly reveal Francis's ambivalence to the press. *High Stakes* has its hero unjustly abused by the press because he fires his crooked trainer. *Smokescreen*'s Edward Link must escape a carefully set-up compromising situation arranged by a two-faced newspaperman. *Banker*'s plot is periodically stirred by dirty accusations leveled by *What's Going On?*, a sleazy financial paper, and *The Danger* and *Trial Run* show the main characters going to great lengths to avoid the damage that journalism can do. Besides *Break In*, however, the best example is *Nerve*, which emphasizes not just the pernicious power of print but the unseemly possibilities of television reporting. In *Break In* and *Bolt*, Kit's love interest is a television newsperson, so there is little criticized about it except its inclination to the visually spectacular. Kit even uses the skillful editing of a videotape to engineer Maynard's entrapment at the conclusion of *Break In*. *Nerve*, however, one of Francis's earliest and best novels, shows television to be as corruptible a medium as print.

Abusing the Airwaves

The beginning of *Nerve* is an immediate grabber; a jockey named Art Mathews shoots himself "loudly and messily" in the parade ring at Dunstable races. The cool, objective voice of the narrator, Rob Finn, states the facts of this horrific event as casually as Mathews performed it, and it is much more immediately shocking than if it had been written in a more melodramatic style. Besides showing how controlled Rob Finn can be, this is one of Francis's backhand openings; it is not apparent for many pages that anything criminal is going on. One is reminded of the openings of *Dead Cert*, *Blood Sport*, and *Proof* in which accidents are eventually unmasked as murder or the even more backhand openings of *Banker* and *Smokescreen* in which unusual events one expects to be connected to the evildoing are revealed to be in the first case an accident and in the second a movie scene. Only persistent questioning by Finn gradually reveals that Mathews's suicide is really a crime—not a crime that the police can do much about but nonetheless a crime. The perpetrator, as is made clear fairly early in the novel, is Maurice Kemp-Lore, a television celebrity.

"To sparkle from the small screen an entertainer must be positively incandescent in real life," observes Finn, "and Kemp-Lore was no exception" (42). Dazzling in person, Kemp-Lore is charming, respected for his interviewing skills, and a fixture on the racing scene. When Finn meets him, Finn is flattered by his offer to appear on "Turf Talk," though he knows Kemp-Lore's effect on him is "calculated," a professional skill he uses on everyone (*N,* 42–43). Like other Francis villains, Kemp-Lore is consumed by his own evil but maintains his public stature with a composed facade. Kemp-Lore gives no indication what he intends to do on the program, remaining vague about what they will discuss, supposedly to preserve spontaneity. First he interviews John Ballerton, a pompous member of the National Hunt Committee, who becomes persuasively genial when being interviewed. Then, as if to comment on a typical jockey's life, Kemp-Lore shows an old film of the inexperienced Finn doing badly in a race. He asks Finn about his background and then abruptly shifts to Finn's finances, which are not very good. He has set Finn up not only to look inept but so that he can elicit a nasty comment from Ballerton and perhaps precipitate an argument. Like newspapers, television needs to stir things up. Ballerton obliges by saying that jockeys complain too much and that most of them are in racing for their egos; they like wearing bright silks (63).

Ballerton has shown himself to be corrupted by equating racing with financial success. He misunderstands the psychology of a good horseman. Finn's ego needs no flattering. Only someone like Ballerton or Kemp-Lore gets involved in racing to build up his ego. Finn replies "truthfully, vehemently, straight from the heart": "Give me a horse and a race to ride it in, and I don't care if I wear silks or . . . or . . . pajamas. . . . I don't care if I earn much money, or if I break my bones, or if I have to starve to keep my weight down. All I care about is racing . . . racing . . . and winning, if I can" (64). Racing is for its own sake, not any of the peripheral benefits, and, ironically in *Nerve,* it is the forced separation from racing that has turned Kemp-Lore bad.

Kemp-Lore comes from a racing family, but asthma forces him to avoid horses. Later the asthma is suggested to be psychosomatic; Kemp-Lore's desire to follow in his father's footsteps became impossible because he feared riding. As the sense of failure festered, he developed an irrational hatred for any successful jockey and works out various psychotic schemes to ruin their careers, especially by rumoring that they have lost their nerve. Besides the vileness of driving a jockey to suicide, Kemp-Lore is fully capable of dressing as a woman, of stealing vehicles and blocking roads to make a jockey late for his rides, of risking his health by fondling horses in order to dope them, and of stringing Finn up by his wrists and leaving him to die.

Kemp-Lore's evil is not only opposed to Finn's goodness but is parallel to it. Kemp-Lore cannot accept his fate. He has no reason to nurse his envy. His life is easier than most jockeys', and he does his television job better than anyone else. Finn, on the other hand, has adjusted to his fate. His family are all musicians, but the lavish talent has not descended to him. None of his family really approves of jockeydom, his uncle calling it a "peculiar pursuit." Finn is bothered by this separation from his family. He is uncomfortable around his father, mother, and uncle. Though he admires his mother, he makes it quite plain that he feels coldness coming from her, and early in the novel when the family begins to play a "jigging piece for strings and woodwind" together, Finn finds listening intolerable and leaves (24).

Finn has a cross to bear, but he is resigned to his fate. It is not any easier than bearing a crushed hand or a crippled wife, and yet, like other Francis heroes, he bears it as well as he can. It is not any easier than coming from a family of horsemen and being unable to ride either, but something in Kemp-Lore has made bearing that cross impossible. He turns it inward and uses it to inflict pain on others so subtly that no one recognizes him as the force behind the seemingly disconnected, unfortunate incidents. The evil destroys not only his chosen victims but has consumed him. Wishing for the impossible, unrealistically refusing to accept one's fate is a prescription for distortion and disaster.

The Italianate Gentleman

One of the few criticisms directed against Francis in his early novel-writing career was that as soon as a character appeared with a hyphenated name, one could be certain that he was the villain. This ignores the fact that in many of Francis's novels (such as *Nerve, High Stakes, Break*

In, and *Bolt*), the question is not so much "Who done it?" but "How will the hero effect justice?" Frequently the malefactor is revealed well before the novel is half over. The hard-boiled mystery does not emphasize the puzzle of the crime as much as the hero's ability to persevere in his quest for justice. As one might expect, therefore, Francis's evildoers are not nearly as subtly drawn as his heroes. The criminal mind is not important to Francis. Men trying to cope with adversity are. Criminals are forces against which the chivalrous protagonist must do battle, and they might as well be Grendel, the Green Knight, or a Jabberwocky.

A survey of the gallery of Francis's "bad guys" reveals a fairly reliable pattern I have come to call the *Italianate gentleman,* a term borrowed from Renaissance English literature. Italy was, of course, the center of western European culture in the Renaissance, and English gentlemen, in order to further their education, traveled to Verona, Venice, Florence, and other cities (the reason so many of these places appear in Shakespeare, though the Bard undoubtedly never visited them himself). Then, as now, it was possible for certain people to be educated beyond their intelligence, and these gentlemen reappeared in their native land as vain, superficial, overly mannered courtiers, which were contrasted with the sturdy English types who were not corrupted by the hifalutin manners, Machiavellian intrigues, and Roman Catholicism of the south. Italianate gentlemen were lampooned or excoriated in the writings of the time and set up the pattern for the traditional British distaste for "Mediterranean types," especially the French. Now, a colonel with a handlebar mustache tsk-tsking over Italian insouciance or disorder is a stock comic character in British comedy, but it would not be funny if it were not based on something ingrained and immediately recognizable in the English character. As Lord Henry Grey of *Flying Finish* puts it: "I was startled and amused at the same time, hearing an echo of my diehard father. 'Wogs begin at Calais' " (87).

Francis's villains regularly share certain traits reminiscent of the Italianate pattern. They are often well heeled, well educated, and well mannered. They often have soft hands or damp handshakes. To the public, they are paragons. The hyphenated names Francis used too frequently in his early novels were deliberate attempts to play upon the public desire for the upper classes to be above certain types of meanness. Francis told an interviewer, "I like my heroes to have an ordinary name. I don't want them to stand out, and if you give the villains aristocratic names, people don't immediately have suspicions about them."[12] This evidently led to Kemp-Lore, George Ellery-Penn (*Dead Cert*), John

Rous-Wheeler *(Flying Finish),* and Charles Carthy-Todd *(Rat Race).* Other aristocrats involved in crime include Lord Vaughnley. All these gentlemen have been corrupted, and their public face conceals the blackness inside. Usually their motivations are not tangled. Greed is their most frequent motive; one needs money to keep up a gentlemanly front. Kemp-Lore, with his psychological motivations, is about the most complex bad character that Francis draws.

When the villain is not a straightforward aristocrat, he often nonetheless has "Italianate" qualities, though he may be no gentleman. John C. Carr asked Francis whether English people would really have been as nasty to Sid Halley as they were in *Odds Against.* Francis replied, "Probably not. But there are different characters about. Latin characters come over here and some Mediterranneans can be very nasty."[13] In other words, even if the English are not really nasty, in general, it takes all sorts to make a world, and some English are as bad as some Mediterraneans. A few of his villains are specifically Italian. *Bonecrack* features Enso Rivera, probably mad from syphilis, who is capable of incredible brutality in order to ensure that his son has good horses to ride. *Twice Shy* has Harry Gilbert and his son, Angelo, who is the "Italian-looking" psychopath of his family. The Gilberts are born in England but of Italian descent. *The Danger's* Pietro Goldoni is the brains behind the kidnappings, a criminal activity common in Italy. The question naturally arises from these repetitions whether Francis is inadvertently using stereotypes as a shortcut to characterization. Perhaps so. Since *The Danger* takes place partly in Italy and has so many Italian characters, it is a good place to start for clues to his attitude, particularly among characters not intended to be villains.

In the opening sequence, Andrew Douglas of Liberty Market Ltd. is in the middle of a stakeout in a hostage situation. Liberty Market is a company that helps wealthy clients with personal security, especially kidnapping, and works for the safe release of kidnap victims. The hostage situation Douglas and the Bolognese police are now faced with has resulted from the vain bungling of the carabinieri. "Stupid, swollen-headed, lethal human failing," Douglas calls it (9), a line Francis might well apply not just to his bunglers but also to his petty criminals, whom he looks on with more of a shake of the head than disgust. "Lethal human failings," especially vanity, are universal and not limited to Italians, although Douglas's description of the carabinieri charging the ransom drop in such numbers that they lose track of the kidnappers sounds rather like the usual chaos frequently ascribed to Italian organi-

zations. The chief Bolognese inspector, Enrico Pucinelli, was off duty
when the "screw-up" [sic] occurred, and when he returns, Francis
portrays him in a seemingly positive manner. Pucinelli is "thin and
forty, give or take. Dark and intense and energetic. A communist in
a communist city, disapproving of the capitalist whose daughter was
at risk" (7). Pucinelli does his duty, regardless of his personal feelings.
Like the Norwegian communist driver-translator in *Slayride* who assists
David Cleveland, he does not let his politics interfere with his profession.
Such professionalism is always a positive trait in Francis. Pucinelli,
however, as a policeman, is also obligated to defer to proper authority.
He must go to his superiors to request an airplane for the hostage
takers and will not assume responsibilities that are not ordinarily part
of his job.

Pucinelli is emotional, especially concerning children. When he discovers the kidnappers have children as hostages, "in one instant he
cared more for them than he had in five weeks for the [kidnapped]
girl, and for the first time, I [Douglas] saw real concern in his olive
face" (13). Later in a restaurant, Pucinelli speaks of his daughters with
"a glimmer in the eyes" (43). He even allows one of the hostage takers
a few moments to hold a little girl on his knee because the crook has
a child of his own that age and might never be able to hold her again.
"Pucinelli like all Italians," observes Douglas, "liked children, and even
carabinieri, I supposed, could be sentimental" (76). This Mediterranean
emotionalism has two sides, however. When Pucinelli states that Douglas
is like all the English, "so cold" (8), and that his head is "like ice"
(76), the reader knows that once again a Francis hero will have trouble
expressing his emotions, and we tend to favor Pucinelli as a more
human character. Douglas cannot help but admire Pucinelli's considerable
personal courage that comes from his concern for the victims of the
hostage takers. Pucinelli walks into the street "exposing his whole body
to the still-present threat of the guns in the apartment" (73). The
psychiatrists on the scene shake their heads, and Douglas admiringly
wonders whether he would have similar courage. The results, however,
are safe children and the criminals' giving up without a fight. It is also
shown that the coldest analysis of an angry hostage taker or a heated
kidnap situation will be the most likely way to get people out alive.
Good stiff-upper-lip British professionalism is far more effective than
high emotion.

That Pucinelli is admirable, even lovable, there is no doubt. Yet
when Douglas goes to England and works with Detective Superintendent

Eagler, he compares the English policeman to the Italian: "He [Eagler] shook my hand limply as if sealing a bargain, as different from Pucinelli as a tortoise from a hare: one wily, one sharp; one wrinkled in his carapace, one leanly taut in his uniform; one always on the edge of his nerves, one avuncularly relaxed. I thought that I would rather be hunted by Pucinelli, any day" (191). This is not very flattering to say about a cop, despite all he does for Douglas. In the end, in fact, he proves more effective at breaking the kidnapping ring than does Eagler. The clichés for Italians are immediately recognizable, and here Francis is not portraying a criminal. There is a kind of awe for Eagler, who is not nearly as obviously feeling as Pucinelli, but, after all, it is those very English qualities, his particular set of clichés, that make him the better hunter.

There is another detective superintendent in the book who is British but ineffective. His name, Rightsworth, implies his character. Douglas says: "Rightsworth gave me barely a nod, and that more of repression than of acknowledgement. One of those, I thought. A civilian-hater. One who thought of the police as 'us' and the public as 'them,' the 'them' being naturally inferior. It always surprised me that policemen of that kind got promoted, but Rightsworth was proof enough that they did" (193). This is about as harsh as Francis ever gets with the British constabulary. If a nasty incident ever comes up about them, the hero usually immediately says something like, "Most of them are actually good men." Rightsworth proves ineffective to a greater degree than anyone else in the novel—British, Italian, or American—so it would be unfair to charge Francis with being prejudiced. Sympathetic characters are of all nationalities and races in the novels, as well as unsympathetic characters. The Cenci family in *The Danger* is a mixed bag with a nasty sister, a good, beautiful, and talented sister, and an admirable (and emotional) nobleman father. Antonio Perelli of *Forfeit* is intelligent, resourceful, and wise.

Yet there is a slight tendency in characterization to rely on standard attributes of various nationalities and classes, which perhaps led one *Punch* reviewer to remark that *Forfeit* was a "harmless bit of racism" because of its portrayal of the sexually liberated, passionate mulatto who is Tyrone's lover.[14] This stereotyping particularly manifests itself in the villains, who are not as carefully drawn as the heroes. Despite Francis's admiration for upper-class values, there is frequently in his characterizations a twinge of distaste for overly sophisticated upper-class people, and they are frequently responsible for tossing the apple into

Eden or at least are indifferent or cynical to it. There is also a rather consistent admiration for sturdy yeoman types, who despite the lack of an education or other advantages can be counted on to do what is right. There is a tendency for the former to be foreign, though the latter may be American, Australian, or other hardy souls who are not necessarily British. The Italianate gentlemen responsible for so much ill in Francis are perhaps little more than the result of his romantic, pastoral ideal of racing, an idyllic view worthy of Constable. People are good when they are plain folk, and even Francis's wealthier or nobler characters, like Tim Ekaterin and Lord Henry Grey, go to great lengths to prove they are "just one of the guys." There is no real evidence of any racism, though Francis may occasionally latch on to a convenient stereotype.

Conclusion

To suggest that Francis's villains are among the weakest links in his chain of absorbing thrillers may be missing the moral objectives of the novels. The bad guys do run too much to type and lack much subtlety; however, the mysteries are still essentially absorbing, and readers overlook this flaw because of Francis's worldview, the moral setup. The villains are less human than allegorical. They represent the force of evil. The hero must be more realistic, for the books are not simply about good's metaphysical struggle with evil, and when the hero is too obviously good, the result is usually a disappointing novel. Good is the assumption; that is, people are born good but must struggle against the corrupting forces in the world.

It is very important, therefore, that the hero be ordinary at the same time he is extraordinary. He is the former because he is subject to most of the humiliations and ill fortune that life may throw. Whether an executive or a jockey, successful or borderline, he is neither fearless nor indestructible nor immune to common emotion. He is extraordinary, however, because of his acceptance of his situation. He sees himself clearly, without self-deception, and, though he may be tempted by money or vanity, he is remarkably effective in resisting. He is sensible and compromising but knows when compromise would lead to the total loss of integrity. In a sense, each novel is a morality play, and in each case, Everyman does battle with evil. He cannot defeat it—it is always just over the horizon—but he can resist it, defeat its minions, and do the best an ordinary man can do in the circumstances. The ideal world where racing people do not get overly obsessed with the secondary aspects, such as profit, cannot exist, but that does not mean that the hero cannot, sometimes absurdly, seek to live according to his vision of that ideal world. The existential choice is what the ordinary man makes against the inevitable incursions of darkness.

Chapter Six
Postscript
The Short Stories

With his schedule as a novelist, it is not surprising that Francis has not written more short stories. Yet he has tried a few pieces of short fiction, and they are quite remarkable in the context of his other work. Most of this book has been devoted to characterizing the Francis formula, and, therefore, most attention has been paid to those elements Francis usually reprises from novel to novel and how he varies them. In his short stories, while retaining some of the typical elements, he has been much freer with narrative technique than he has ever been in a novel. The short stories are connected to racing, and they repeat the themes of existential responsibility and of fathers and sons, but in technique they are quite different.

The best is the story published under the titles "The Big Story" and "A Day of Wine and Roses."[1] Taking place at the Kentucky Derby, the story tells of a reporter whose reputation is keeping him from being fired for alcoholism. The Derby is his last chance. If he botches the job, his career will be over. Typical Francis elements are plain. The protagonist has a cross to bear. He is suffering from the mental inertia that often afflicts Francis's heroes. The ambiguities of the profession of journalism are suggested. This story, however, departs greatly from the novels. First, the story is told in third person, whereas all of the novels are first person. It also shifts point of view through a number of characters, including the writer Fred Collyer, his editor, the crooked jockey, the race fixer, and even a pickpocket who has come to Churchill Downs to work the crowd. Only once in his two dozen novels has Francis used more than one point of view. In that instance, however, *Twice Shy* was split into two large sections in which each of two brothers narrated their parts of the larger tale in a manner not notably different from other Francis protagonists. What "The Big Story" achieves by this caroming among characters is a feeling for the variety of people at Churchill Downs on racing day and proves that Francis is much more capable of imagining the criminal mind than he credits himself. The mystery itself becomes secondary to the fascinations of these different characters and to the theme of the random effects people have upon one another. The minor league pickpocket, for example, steals Collyer's wallet, thus preventing his drinking for a while and allowing Collyer to put together the "big story." Fate intervenes, it seems, to save Collyer from himself, but later, when he crawls back into the bottle, the implication is once again that though happenstance may affect lives, certain choices are ultimately in the hands of their possessors. Only Fred Collyer, by a strong act of will, can save himself from his alcoholism.

The second major difference from the novels is that Collyer, the central figure, is no hero. Throughout this book, I have referred to Francis's narrators as "the hero," and the term certainly applies to Sid Halley, Jonah Dereham, and all the rest. It does not apply to Collyer. He fails abysmally, and there is no indication that the criminals will ever be caught. In a Francis novel, Collyer would be a minor, pathetic character, like Bert Checkov or Crispin Dereham—someone who is contrasted to the more active and willful hero. Perhaps Francis feels it would be difficult to sustain interest in such an antihero for three hundred pages, although he certainly accomplishes it in the story. Shifting Collyer to center stage results in a lessening of the moral paradigm that is so important in the novels and creates more of an effect of a slice of life. The realism gives "The Big Story" a rawness that other Francis works often lack. The usual optimism is buried under the irony, and the literary quality of the story is yet another proof of Francis's extraordinary capabilities. He has threatened to produce a novel that has no connection to horses (which gives his publisher a jolt), and the talent obvious in this story—not to mention the novels—proves him more than capable.

Martin Retsov, the protagonist of "Nightmares," is also a failure, but Retsov is a criminal.[2] Like "The Big Story," "Nightmares" is a third-person narrative, but it adheres strictly to Retsov's point of view. The trick ending, in fact, would not work without using the limited point of view, but the story shows, despite Francis's protestations to the contrary, that he is able to slip into the criminal mind. Most criminal minds, after all, are only slightly bent normal minds. The story captures the feeling of the banality of crime also. Retsov's plotting is not intense, vicious, or passionate. He goes through his plans methodically, forcing a hitchhiker to be his assistant, arranging for a horse

box, and setting up a potential buyer for the stolen brood mare. The
main detective in this story is ghostly and ominous, an anonymous
spectre out of Martin's worst nightmare. Most of the emotion focuses
on something much more recognizable as a Francis trait, the relationship
between father and son.

Retsov has a cross to bear: he killed his father. It was an accident,
but the nightmares of the title all come from his memory of trying to
escape from the police by redirecting a horse box through an opening
between a patrol car and a fence. In backing up, he ran over his father.
As fathers go in Francis, the elder Retsov was a good parent, with the
significant exception that he had trained his son to be a horse thief.
Old Retsov was even good at his criminal work, so he has the positive
trait of professionalism. Martin cannot carry on the trade without a
partner, and finding one as skilled as the elder Retsov is not easy.
When Martin coerces the hitchhiker into becoming his aide, he assumes
a parental role, teaching the young man the details of his trade. As
Martin, in a sense, betrayed his father by backing up carelessly in trying
to drive away, the young man betrays Martin. Once again Francis
produces a disturbing view of the ties between father and son.

"A Carrot for a Chestnut" reprises this theme, though it does not
fully reveal this aspect of the story until the O. Henry–like surprise
ending.[3] The surprise cheapens this story somewhat, and overall it is
the least successful of his stories. Again Francis puts the story in third
person, with most of it in the main character's mind. Unlike "Nightmares," however, he does not use a limited point of view and shifts
among several characters. This technique, which works well in creating
the atmosphere for "The Big Story," is not as successful here. The
shifts are sudden sometimes and insubstantial. There seems no reason
to go into the veterinarian's mind or into Toddy Morrison's for only
a few lines. The man who hires Chick to dope a horse could just as
well have remained the shadowy figure he was at the beginning of the
story, and his guilt over the results of his plot serves no useful purpose
in the story except to show that Francis can get into a criminal mind
and to allow the contrast between the innocent great-hearted horse and
corruptible mankind to be developed more.

Chick's personality is what is important in this story, and some of
these other points of view are merely distractions. Chick is indecisive
but arrogant. He refuses to take responsibility for himself and feels the
world owes him something. He deludes himself into thinking he always
knows more than the people around him. When he agrees to the

criminal act, he does so by blaming everyone around him for forcing him to it. Even the act itself—feeding a carrot stuffed with drugs to a horse—is enough of an active choice that he has great difficulty carrying it out. When faced with the reality that his delayed giving of the carrot will result in the horse's appearing fit enough to run, Chick wrangles with himself over whether to tell. He is not even able to decide not to tell; the race begins while he vacillates. By contrast, Toddy Morrison is described as having rejected his father's attitude to life, but instead of stewing over it, he left home to ride for other trainers, thus becoming a man and gaining Arthur Morrison's respect. Arthur is one of those fathers who temper the steel in their sons by fire. Arthur and Toddy have a relationship reminiscent of the Griffons' in *Bonecrack,* only the Morrisons have managed to come back together on new terms. Chick will never have a good relationship with his father because he cannot assert his own manhood. He is unprofessional and cussedly unwilling to accept reality. The final scene in which Chick lies in a hospital bed paralyzed is symbolic of his life before the accident. By refusing to take responsibility for himself, he has put himself in a "No Exit" situation in which all he can do is insult others for his own problems brought on himself. He cannot even enjoy the £300 he earned for his crime.

"Twenty-one Men Good and True" is a satisfying tale of rigged betting with a good trick ending.[4] Its narrative technique is similar to "The Big Story" in shifting among several characters. Again Francis shows he is capable of getting into a criminal's head, and in this case there is even a certain admiration for the professional, not very greedy, behavior of the crook who sets up the foolproof betting scheme. Arnold Roper takes twenty-five pounds sterling from each member of his staff of twenty-one punters; they take all the rest of the winnings. He lives in simple, even tawdry, surroundings, surrounded by his stashes of money. The most strongly depicted character, however, is Jamie Finland, an innocent blind boy who stumbles on the scheme. Jamie's life is vividly and sympathetically portrayed. He rises in the morning and listens to his mother's taped note. He senses colors. He listens to a half-dozen radios and a "telly." He is seemingly happy, and a reader cheers with him when he wins his first bet. The depiction is free of bathos, free of pity, and Jamie has what many of the novel heroes lack initially: comfortable acceptance of the conditions fate has given. There is a sort of ironic bemusement, for example, when Jamie imagines that sound without pictures is almost as bad for his mother as pictures without sound would be for him. He even considers himself lucky, "in the material stakes." Although there is no mention of a father, what is shown of his mother is hard working and also strong against adversity. She too can accept life's prickles. By the end of the story, I am a good deal sorry that Jamie is going to lose—in fact be the unwitting undoing of—the scheme that could so easily give mother and son extra comfort.

Other characters whose points of view are represented are less vivid but once again give the impression of the range of humanity in the racing game. Billy Hitchins, a young and talented bookmaker who turned his mathematical talents from the academic to the gambling business; the starter; and the judge who pores over photos of tight finishes and may get unjustly accused of the crime are three such characters. Each is doing his job, trying to get by, the judge and the starter mainly worried about what other people will think of their performance while Billy frets about profits. Greg Simpson, one of Roper's agents, occupies a large chunk of the story, mostly to show how the betting portion of the scheme works. He is another Francis reminder of the corruptibility of human beings. He exchanges his principles for the chance to make easy money. A fifty-two-year-old managerial employee tossed out of his job by mergers and cutbacks, Simpson's inability to get another job and the humiliations of a declining income make him willing not only to become part of the scheme but to remain happily ignorant of most of its workings. His ambitions, like Arnold Roper's, are relatively benign. Maybe he will be able to afford a new car, and maybe his wife will be able to book the ski holiday with the children. On the other hand he has given up his principles because he is unable to accept the life-style forced retirement has shoved him toward. The banality of evil is once again portrayed. Instead of the quintessentially evil masterminds who recur through the novels, the stories emphasize convincing portraits of petty schemers. This, and the interesting variations with point of view, prove clearly that there are many more talents in Francis's stable than he is often given credit for.

Summing Up

What better praise can be given a popular writer than that millions of people enjoy his work? This, perhaps: that he does not cheapen sensation, pander, or diminish the power of his art. All of this is true of Dick Francis. His writings are a high-wire act. They hold an impressive balance over enormous canyons. They are violent but not titillating.

They are moral but not oppressive. They are formulaic but not repetitive. They are didactic but not dull. The prose is plain but not pretentiously so. The themes center on manhood but are not chauvinistic. The protagonists are heroic but not superhuman. Realism is his objective, yet he does not take away the fantasies. Francis proves annually that to be moderate is not necessarily to be mediocre and to be entertaining is not necessarily to be tawdry. There rages still an ongoing debate on whether certain films, television, and writings are harmful to those who consume them. I cannot be certain that this is not so. Of this, however, I am certain: no one is a worse person for having read Dick Francis, and I sincerely suspect we are all made a bit more determined to do better against adversity.

Notes and References

Chapter One

1. Unless otherwise indicated, the biographical details that follow are from Francis's autobiography, *The Sport of Queens* (New York: Penzler, 1957; revised 1982); hereafter abbreviated *SQ* and cited parenthetically in the text.

2. Robert Cantwell, "Mystery Makes a Writer," *Sports Illustrated*, 25 March 1968, 81.

3. *Smokescreen* (New York: Pocket Books, 1972), 23.

4. "Dick Francis," *New Yorker*, 15 March 1969, 30.

5. Cantwell, "Mystery Makes a Writer," 78.

6. Pete Axthelm, "Writer with a Whip Hand," *Newsweek*, 6 April 1981, 99.

7. John C. Carr, "Dick Francis" (interview), in *The Craft of Crime* (Boston: Houghton Mifflin, 1983), 206.

8. "Authors and Editors," *Publishers' Weekly*, 8 January 1968, 27.

9. *New Yorker*, 30.

10. Cantwell, "Mystery Makes a Writer," 87.

11. Red Smith, "Cherchez a Horsethief Who Reads," *New York Times*, 4 July 1977, 7.

12. Jack Newcombe, "Jockey with an Eye for Intrigue," *Life*, 6 June 1969, 82.

13. Edward Zuckerman, "Dick Francis," *New York Times Magazine*, 25 March 1984, 60.

14. Ibid.

15. Carr, "Dick Francis," 225.

16. Dick Francis, "Writing Mystery Novels: An Interview by Brigitte Weeks," *Writer* (August 1983): 12.

17. Zuckerman, "Dick Francis," 54.

18. Ibid.

19. Gerald H. Strauss, "Dick Francis," in *Beacham's Popular Fiction in America*, Series I (Washington, D.C.: Research Publishing, 1986), 467.

20. Zuckerman, "Dick Francis," 54.

21. Axthelm, "Writer with a Whip Hand," 100.

22. Kenneth Clark, *The Romantic Rebellion* (New York: Harper & Row, 1973), 234.

23. Edwin McDowell, "Teamwork," *New York Times Book Review*, 12 April 1981, 47.

24. John Leonard, "Books of the Times," *New York Times*, 20 March 1981, sec. III, 25.

25. Diana Cooper-Clark, "Interview with Dick Francis," in *Designs of Darkness* (Bowling Green, Ohio: Bowling Green University Popular Press, 1983), 239.

26. Judy Klemesrud, "Behind the Best Sellers," *New York Times Book Review*, 1 June 1980, 42.

27. *New Yorker*, 30.

28. Axthelm, "Writer with a Whip Hand," 99–100.

29. Zuckerman, "Dick Francis," 54.

30. Ibid.

31. Carr, "Dick Francis," 224.

32. Klemesrud, "Behind the Best Sellers," 42.

33. Axthelm, "Writer with a Whip Hand," 100.

34. Cantwell, "Mystery Makes a Writer," 87. A similar description of Francis's writing discipline is in Mort Hochstein, "Dick Francis, Odds-on Favorite," *Writer's Digest* (August 1986): 32–34.

Chapter Two

1. Cooper-Clark, "Interview with Dick Francis," 225–26. Francis seems to think of the "British mystery" with its emphasis on plot and puzzle when the term *mystery* is used and, since he avoids detective protagonists, does not think of himself as writing "detective" novels. He is, I think, minimizing similarities to emphasize the individuality of his own form.

2. Francis, "Writing Mystery Novels," 12. A fine overview of the Francis hero is given in Barry Baushka's "Endure and Prevail: The Novels of Dick Francis," *Armchair Detective* 11 (1978): 238–44. Many of the points made in this chapter are similar, but not identical, to Baushka's, and he, of course, did not have the opportunity to go into the same depth. It is nonetheless one of the best articles on Francis to date.

3. Raymond Chandler, "The Simple Art of Murder: An Essay," in *The Simple Art of Murder* (New York: Ballantine, 1950), 1–21.

4. Ibid., 20–21.

5. *Dead Cert* (New York: Pocket Books, 1962), 44; hereafter abbreviated *DC* and cited parenthetically in the text.

6. Francis, "Writing Mystery Novels," 12.

7. Cooper-Clark, "An Interview with Dick Francis," 226.

8. Ibid., 232.

9. Francis, "Writing Mystery Novels," 12.

10. Cooper-Clark, "An Interview with Dick Francis," 226.

11. *Odds Against;* in *Three to Show* (New York: Harper & Row, 1969), 444–661; hereafter abbreviated *OA* and cited parenthetically in the text.

12. "I try to give my heroes a cross to bear because I don't consider myself first and foremost a novelist," he has said (Cooper-Clark, "An Interview with Dick Francis," 230), once again asserting that such a detail helps fill

up the book. Whatever his reason for doing so, it creates the effects discussed subsequently.

13. "I usually have a main character who has to fight his way out of tight corners and this main character is learning things all along," Ibid., 225.

14. *Whip Hand* (New York: Pocket Books, 1979), 76; hereafter abbreviated *WH* and cited parenthetically in the text.

15. Woody Allen, "Mr. Big," in *Getting Even* (New York: Random House, 1971), 139–51.

16. Examples include the situation of Garcin in the play *No Exit*, with its famous line "Hell is—other people!" (*No Exit and Three Other Plays* [New York: Vintage, 1955], 47) or the following words from *St. Genet: Actor and Martyr* (in *Existentialism*, ed. Robert C. Solomon [New York: Modern Library, 1974], 239): "Here is a man being dragged along by two cops: 'What has he done?' I ask. 'He's a crook,' answer the cops. The word strikes against its object like a crystal falling into a supersaturated solution. The solution immediately crystallizes, enclosing the word inside itself. In prose, the word dies so that the object may be born. 'He's a crook!' I forget the word then and there, I see I touch, I breathe a crook; with all my senses I feel that secret substance: crime."

17. *For Kicks* (New York: Pocket Books, 1965), 17; hereafter abbreviated *FK* and cited parenthetically in the text.

18. Cooper-Clark, "An Interview with Dick Francis," 231.

Chapter Three

1. Francis, "Writing Mystery Novels," 11.

2. Cooper-Clark, "An Interview with Dick Francis," 236.

3. Carr, "Dick Francis," 213.

4. *Banker* (New York: Fawcett Crest, 1982), 22; hereafter cited parenthetically in the text.

5. *Risk* (New York: Harper & Row, 1977), 100; hereafter cited parenthetically in the text.

6. *In the Frame* (New York: Pocket Books, 1976), 49; hereafter cited parenthetically in the text.

7. *Nerve* (New York: Pocket Books, 1964), 24; hereafter cited parenthetically in the text.

8. *Flying Finish* (New York: Pocket Books, 1966), 114; hereafter abbreviated as *FF* and cited parenthetically in the text.

9. Michael Stanton discusses *Bonecrack* in relation to its accord with the theme of the salvation of love, which I discuss in chapter 4. Stanton is a bit more optimistic about the effect of the alienation between father and son than I am, but he makes a number of excellent points. "Dick Francis: The Worth of Human Love," *Armchair Detective* 15 (1982): 142–143.

10. *Bonecrack* (New York: Harper & Row, 1971), 30; hereafter cited parenthetically in the text.

11. *Reflex* (New York: G. P. Putnam's Sons, 1981), 44; hereafter abbreviated as *Re* and cited parenthetically in the text.

12. *Enquiry* (New York: Pocket Books, 1969), 96; hereafter cited parenthetically in the text.

Chapter Four

1. *Bloomsbury Review* 7, no. 3 (May–June 1987):13, recently offered a review by Glenda Burnside of two novels published by small presses that feature lesbian detectives: Katherine V. Forrest, *Murder at the Nightwood Bar* (Tallahassee: Naiad Press, 1987), and Barbara Wilson, *Sisters of the Road* (Seattle: Seal Press, 1987). Forrest's novel is set in Los Angeles, though it is described as more a "police procedural" than "hard-boiled."

2. Female boxing has appeared periodically, surrounded by the bemused publicity that indicates most reporters think it bizarre, kinky, and exotic. All the same, even the mass media have experimented with the interesting variation of the physically tough woman. What man in his thirties does not with pleasure remember Mrs. Peel of "The Avengers"? Just at the prepubescent age when men of my generation thought we had television (and therefore the universe) sorted out, along came "The Avengers." Who can forget the shock and erotic thrill of first seeing Mrs. Peel karate kick a bully senseless? Of course, we would later be reassured by Emma's being softly dressed and sipping champagne with the urbane Steed, but we could never look at a woman the same way. By the time the film *Alien* came along, one was surprised and delighted, but not particularly stunned, that in such a traditional form as the horror movie it was a woman who proved to be the creature's only worthy opponent.

3. Marty S. Knepper, "Dick Francis," in *Twelve Englishmen of Mystery,* ed. Earl F. Bargannier (Bowling Green, Ohio: Bowling Green University Popular Press, 1984), 226.

4. Amanda Cross [pseud. Carolyn Heilbrun], *The Question of Max* (New York: Knopf, 1976), 117, cited by ibid., 248, n.3.

5. *Knockdown* (London: Pan, 1974), 39; hereafter cited parenthetically in the text.

6. *The Danger* (New York: Fawcett Crest, 1984), 120; hereafter cited parenthetically in the text.

7. *Rat Race* (New York: Pocket Books, 1971), 18; hereafter cited parenthetically in the text.

8. Henry James, *The Ambassadors,* ed. R. W. Stallman (New York: Signet, 1960), 134.

9. *Twice Shy* (New York: Fawcett Crest, 1982), 117; hereafter cited parenthetically in the text.

10. *Forfeit* (New York: Harper and Row, 1969), 51; hereafter cited parenthetically in the text.

11. *Blood Sport* (New York: Pocket Books, 1967), 47; hereafter cited parenthetically in the text.

12. *Slayride* (New York: Pocket Books, 1973), 24; hereafter abbreviated as *SL* and cited parenthetically in the text.

13. Particularly by Knepper, "Dick Francis."

14. Baushka, "Endure and Prevail."

Chapter Five

1. Judith Rascoe, "On Vicarious Danger," *Christian Science Monitor*, 17 July 1969, 11.

2. Cooper-Clark, "An Interview with Dick Francis," p. 234.

3. Christopher Lehmann-Haupt, *New York Times*, 27 March 1986, sec. III, 23; Marilyn Stasio, "Back on the Track," *New York Times*, 16 March 1986, sec. VII, 7. Martha Duffy, another reviewer, asked, "Dick Francis, won't you please go home?" in exasperation at his "wanderlust" that led him to write about locations away from the British race track: "Francis, Go Home," *Time*, 5 March 1973, 75-Ell. While I agree with her that *Smokescreen* is not one of Francis's best, I wonder about the general advice implicit in the comments. She misses the point. If Francis had ground out one British jockey after another, a succession of Sid Halley clones, would anyone much be interested in his newest novel? *Break In* is not a triumph because it takes place at the track, nor is *Smokescreen* a dud simply because it takes place in Africa. Francis has a right to branch out, and doing so has produced novels as good as, if not better than, some of the racing books.

4. T. E. D. Klein, horror writer and former editor of *Twilight Zone* magazine, made the observation in a presentation at Pennsylvania State University in Erie (19 March 1987) that all horror stories boiled down to the statement, "The supernatural exists." This distinguishes them from the mysteries, which deny the supernatural. The murderer always escapes from the classic "locked room" in a logical way.

5. *Break In* (New York: Putnam's 1986), 63; hereafter abbreviated as *BI* and cited parenthetically in the text.

6. *Bolt* (New York: Putnam's, 1987), 46; hereafter abbreviated *Bo* and cited parenthetically in the text.

7. One might observe that the mystery in general is a form of comedy not because it is humorous but because it usually uses the structure of stasis-disruption-stasis, avoiding Aristotle's "pity and terror," catharsis, and the creation of tragic heroes. This, I suspect, is another reason mysteries are—despite copious carnage—favorite bedtime reading.

8. Cooper-Clark, "An Interview with Dick Francis," 233.

9. *Proof* (New York: Fawcett Crest, 1985), 82; hereafter cited parenthetically in the text.

10. "West 57th," CBS-TV, 20 April 1987. I am surprised Francis has yet to use the occupation of equine mortality investigator in one of his novels.

11. Carr, "Dick Francis," 220–21.

12. Ibid., 214.

13. Ibid., 223.

14. Leo Harris, "Unlawful Assembly," *Punch* 22 (January 1969): 143.

Chapter Six

1. "The Big Story," in *Ellery Queen's Crime Wave,* ed. Ellery Queen (New York: Putnam, 1976), 281–302; "A Day of Wine and Roses," *Sports Illustrated* 7 May 1973, 106–12, 116–19.

2. "Nightmares," in *Ellery Queen's Searches and Seizures,* ed. Ellery Queen (New York: Davis, 1977), 141–49.

3. "A Carrot for a Chestnut," *Sports Illustrated,* 5 January 1970, 48–59.

4. "Twenty-one Men Good and True," in *Verdict of 13: A Detection Club Anthology* (New York: Ballantine, 1978), 44–59.

Selected Bibliography

PRIMARY SOURCES

Novels

Banker. New York: Fawcett Crest, 1982.
Blood Sport. New York: Pocket Books, 1967.
Bolt. New York: Putnam's, 1987.
Bonecrack. New York: Harper & Row, 1971.
Break In. New York: Putnam's, 1986.
The Danger. New York: Fawcett Crest, 1984.
Dead Cert. New York: Pocket Books, 1962.
Enquiry. New York: Pocket Books, 1969.
Flying Finish. New York: Pocket Books, 1966.
For Kicks. New York: Pocket Books, 1965.
Forfeit. New York: Harper & Row, 1969.
High Stakes. New York: Pocket Books, 1975.
Hot Money. New York: Putnam's, 1988.
In the Frame. New York: Pocket Books, 1976.
Knockdown. London: Pan, 1974.
Nerve. New York: Pocket Books, 1964.
Odds Against. 1965. In *Three to Show*, pp. 444–661.
Proof. New York: Fawcett Crest, 1985.
The Racing Game. Reprint of *Odds Against*. New York: Pocket Books, 1984.
Rat Race. New York: Pocket Books, 1971.
Reflex. New York: Putnam's, 1981.
Risk. New York: Harper & Row, 1977.
Slayride. New York: Pocket Books, 1973.
Smokescreen. New York: Pocket Books, 1972.
Three to Show [contains *Dead Cert, Nerve,* and *Odds Against*]. New York: Harper & Row, 1969.
Three Winners [contains *Dead Cert, Nerve,* and *For Kicks*]. London: Michael Joseph, 1977.
Trial Run. New York: Pocket Books, 1978.
Twice Shy. New York: Fawcett Crest, 1982.
Two by Francis [contains *Forfeit* and *Slayride*]. New York: Harper & Row, 1983.
Whip Hand. New York: Pocket Books, 1979.

Nonfiction Books

A Jockey's Life: The Biography of Lester Piggott. New York: Putnam's
   Sons, 1986. Published in Britain as *Lester: The Official Biography.*
   London: Michael Joseph, 1986.
The Sport of Queens. New York: Penzler Books, 1957; revised 1981.

Articles

"Can't Anybody Here Write These Games? The Trouble with Sports
   Fiction." *New York Times Book Review,* 1 June 1986, 56.
   Commentary on the shortage of good sports novels.
"Writing Mystery Novels: (An Interview by Brigitte Weeks)." *Washington
   Post (Book World),* 27 March 1983, 10. Reprinted in *Writer* (August
   1983): 11–12. Describes working methods and Francis's view of his
   moral and aesthetic intentions.

Also weekly column in London *Sunday Express,* 1957–73, and various
contributions to *Horseman's Year, In Praise of Hunting,* and *Stud and
Stable.*

Short Fiction

"Carrot for a Chestnut." *Sports Illustrated,* 5 January 1970, 48–59.
   Reprinted in *Stories of Crime and Detection.* Edited by Joan Berbrick.
   New York: McGraw-Hill, 1974. Also in *Ellery Queen's Faces of
   Mystery.* Edited by Ellery Queen. New York: Davis, 1977.
"A Day of Wine and Roses." *Sports Illustrated,* 7 May 1973, 106-12,
   116–19. Reprinted as "The Big Story." In *Ellery Queen's Crime
   Wave.* Edited by Ellery Queen. New York: Putnam, 1976.
"Nightmares." In *Ellery Queen's Searches and Seizures,* 141–49. Edited by
   Ellery Queen. New York: Davis, 1977.
"Twenty-one Men Good and True." In *Verdict of 13: A Detection Club
   Anthology,* 44–59. Introduction by Julian Symons. New York:
   Ballantine, 1978. Reprinted in *Best Detective Stories of the Year:
   1980.* Edited by E. D. Hoch. New York: Dutton, 1980.

Edited Works

Best Racing and Chasing Stories. Edited by Dick Francis and John
   Welcome. London: Faber and Faber, 1966. Selections from Edgar
   Wallace, Julian Symons, Ernest Hemingway, and *Dead Cert,* among
   many others.

Best Racing and Chasing Stories 2. Edited by Dick Francis and John Welcome. London: Faber and Faber, 1969. Anthology similar to volume 1.

The Racing Man's Bedside Book. Edited by Dick Francis and John Welcome. London: Faber and Faber, 1969. Selected writings on horse racing, including excerpts from *The Sport of Queens,* Siegfried Sassoon, Colin Davy, Gordon Richards, and many others.

SECONDARY SOURCES

Articles

"Authors & Editors." *Publishers' Weekly,* 8 January 1968, 27–28. Introduction to Francis upon publication of *Blood Sport.*

Axthelm, Pete. "Writer with a Whip Hand." *Newsweek,* 6 April 1981, 99–100. Biographical material and some discussion of themes.

Bauska, Barry. "Endure and Prevail: The Novels of Dick Francis." *Armchair Detective* 11 (1978): 238–44. Characteristics of Francis's heroes and his moral emphasis.

Beyer, Andrew. "Horses Are Essence of Mystery to Francis." *Washington Post,* 12 April 1984, Bl. Biographical information and how Francis gets ideas.

Cantwell, R. "Mystery Makes a Writer." *Sports Illustrated,* 25 March 1968, 76–88. Excellent profile emphasizing Francis's racing background.

Carr, John C. "Dick Francis" (interview). In *The Craft of Crime,* 202–26. Boston: Houghton Mifflin, 1983. Wide-ranging and excellent interview covers everything from biography to theories of writing.

"Dick Francis: Interview." *New Yorker,* 15 March 1969, 29–30. Dick and Mary talk about their lives.

"Dick Francis." *Current Biography* (1981): 152–56. Summary of Francis's life.

Ginsburg, Ina. "Dick Francis." *Interview* (June 1986): 100. Interview.

Gould, Charles E. "The Reigning Phoenix." *Armchair Detective* 17, no. 4 (1984): 407–10. Meditation on Francis's celebrity.

Hauptfuhrer, Fred. "Sport of Kings? It's the Knaves that Ex-Jockey Dick Francis Writes Thrillers About." *People,* 7 June 1976, 66. Brief description of Francis's biography, work and personal habits, and lifestyle.

Hill, Holly. "Jockey Turned Detective." *Horizon* (April 1981): 6. Brief article on "The Racing Game."

Hochstein, Mort. "Dick Francis, Odds-on Favorite." *Writer's Digest* (August 1986): 32. Discussion of writing methods by Francis.

Kernan, Michael. "Dick Francis' Literary Bloodlines: A Rider's Fall and Rise." *Washington Post,* 6 November 1982, Cl. Profile of Francis done at the thirty-first Washington International.

Klemesrud, Judy. "Behind the Best Sellers: Dick Francis." *New York Times Book Review,* 1 June 1980, 42. Introduction to Francis on publication of *Whip Hand.*

Knepper, Marty S. "Dick Francis." In *Twelve Englishmen of Mystery,* 222–48. Edited by Earl F. Bargainnier. Bowling Green, Ohio: Bowling Green University Popular Press, 1984. Excellent overview of novels emphasizes the theme of risk taking and Francis's own embrace of risk taking in his writing.

Lowenkopf, Shelly. "The Point of No Return (When Major Characters Cannot Retreat From Committed Action)." *Writer* (August 1983): 20. Uses *Reflex* as an example of how the middle of a novel should be written.

McDowell, Edwin. "Teamwork." *New York Times Book Review,* 12 April 1981, 47. Dick talks about his relationship with Mary.

Newcombe, Jack. "Jockey with an Eye for Intrigue." *Life,* 6 June 1969, 81–82. Profile with photographs concentrating on Devon Loch mystery.

"Riding High." *Forbes,* 15 April 1976, 100. Brief profile.

Ross, Jean W. "CA Interview." *Contemporary Authors,* New Revision Series, 9 (1982): 176–78. Interview about life and working methods.

Simross, Lynn. "Mysteries Are a Winning Mount for British Novelist," *Los Angeles Times,* 12 September 1984, sec. V, 1. Interview with biographical and personal information.

Smith, Red. "Cherchez a Horse Thief Who Reads." *New York Times,* 4 July 1977, 1. Discusses coincidence of a real "mare napping" and plot of *Blood Sport.*

Stanton, Michael N. "Dick Francis: The Worth of Human Love." *Armchair Detective* 15, no. 2 (1982): 137–43. Survey of elements characteristic of Francis's novels, with particular attention to the role of values.

Strauss, Gerald. "Dick Francis." In *Popular Fiction in America,* 466–73. Washington, D.C.: Research Publishing, 1986. Overview of Francis's work focusing on *Whip Hand, Banker,* and *Proof.*

Zuckerman, E. "The Winning Form of Dick Francis." *New York Times Magazine,* 25 March 1984, 40–50, 54, 60. Interview and discussion of themes and subjects of novels.

Selected Reviews

Banker
    Atlantic, (May 1983): 105.

New York Times Book Review, 27 March 1983, 15, 20.
New York Times, 6 April 1983, sec. III, 21.
New Yorker, 11 April 1983, 138.
Punch, 6 April 1983, 74.
Times Literary Supplement, 10 December 1982, 1378.

Blood Sport
Book World, 9 March 1969, 378.
Saturday Review, 26 April 1969, 37.

Bolt
Erie Times News, 12 April 1987, 11–K
Observer, 12 October 1986, 29.
New York Times Book Review, 29 March 1987, 22.
People Weekly, 16 March 1987, 14.
Time, 27 April 1987, 83.

Bonecrack
Atlantic (June 1972): 112.
Book World, 16 July 1972, 14.
New Yorker, 22 July 1972, 80.
Saturday Review, 2 December 1972, 82.
Time, 22 May 1972, 96.
Times Literary Supplement, 31 December 1971, 1638.

Break In
Christian Science Monitor, 24 March 1986, 30.
Los Angeles Times Book Review, 6 July 1986, 73.
New York Times, 16 March 1986, sec. VII, 7.
Punch, 9 October 1985, 74.
USA Today, 19 March 1986, 4D.
Wall Street Journal, 4 March 1986, 28.

The Danger
Christian Science Monitor, 25 April 1984, 20.
Los Angeles Times Book Review, 3 June 1984, 16.
New York Times, 16 March 1984, sec. 3, 23.
New Yorker, 16 April 1984, 161.
Wall Street Journal, 16 May 1984, 30.

Enquiry
Atlantic, August 1970, 114.
Saturday Review, 1 August 1970, 29.
Spectator, 22 November 1969, 721.
Times Literary Supplement, 22 January 1970, 93.

Flying Finish
New York Times, 18 June 1967, sec. VII, 35.
New York Times Book Review, 28 September 1975, 38.
Times Literary Supplement, 8 December 1966, 1157.

Saturday Review, 29 July 1967, 29.
Forfeit
   Atlantic (March 1969): 154.
   Christian Science Monitor, 17 July 1969, 11 (also *The Sport of Queens*).
   London Magazine 14, no. 6 (February–March 1975): 142–43.
   New York Times, 27 July 1975, sec. VII, 18.
   New York Times, 6 March 1969: 41 (also *The Sport of Queens*).
   Punch, 22 January 1969, 143.
High Stakes
   New Republic, 26 June 1976, 29.
   New York Times, 13 June 1976, sec. VII, 26.
   New Yorker, 24 May 1976, 156.
   Observer, 26 October 1975, 30.
   Time, 31 May 1976, 67.
   Times Literary Supplement, 31 October 1975, 1285.
In the Frame
   Critic (Fall 1977): 87.
   New Republic, 11 June 1977, 35.
   New York Times, 3 April 1977, sec. VII, 50.
   New Yorker, 2 May 1977, 147.
   Newsweek, 25 April 1977, 92–93.
   Observer, 10 October 1976, 27.
A Jockey's Life. See also *Lester*.
   Publishers' Weekly, 8 August 1986, 64.
Knockdown
   Book World, 8 June 1975, 1.
   New York Times, 13 July 1975, sec. VII, 36.
   New Yorker, 2 June 1975, 112.
   Observer, 3 November 1974, 33.
   Progressive (July 1975): 44.
Lester, The Official Biography
   London Review of Books, 17 April 1986, 9.
   Observer, 20 July 1986, 23.
   Spectator, 29 March 1986, 27.
Proof
   Armchair Detective 19, no. 1 (Winter 1986): 77–78.
   Book World, 17 March 1985, 5.
   New York Times Book Review, 24 March 1985, 13.
   New York Times, 12 March 1985, sec. III, 17.
   Spectator, 5 January 1985, 21.
   Times Literary Supplement, 29 March 1985, 340.
   USA Today, 11 April 1985, 2C.

"The Racing Game" (television)
   New York Times, 8 April 1980, sec. C, 15.
Rat Race
   Book World, 9 July 1972, 7.
   National Review, 24 August 1971, 937.
   New York Times, 7 April 1971, 41.
   Observer, 18 October 1970, 34.
   Times Literary Supplement, 25 December 1970, 1525.
   Saturday Review, 24 April 1971, 43.
Reflex
   Atlantic (May 1981): 84.
   New York Times, 29 March 1981, sec. VII, 3.
   New York Times, 20 March 1981, sec. III, 25.
   New Yorker, 20 April 1981, 156.
   Punch, 14 January 1981, 71.
   Spectator, 18 October 1980, 23.
   Time, 11 May 1981, 90.
   Times Literary Supplement, 10 October 1980, 1127.
Risk
   Book World, 21 May 1978, E6.
   New York Times, 7 July 1978, sec. III, p. 19.
   New York Times, 4 May 1978, sec. 3, p. 21.
   New Yorker, 21 August 1978, 95.
   Saturday Review, 13 May 1978, 41.
   Spectator, 3 December 1977, 32.
Slayride. See also *Forfeit* and *Two by Francis.*
   Book World, 18 August 1974, 2.
   New York Times, 17 February 1974, sec. VII, 33.
   New Yorker, 1 April 1974, 124.
   Observer, 14 October 1973, 38.
   Time, 11 March 1974, 102.
   Times Literary Supplement, 18 January 1974, 61.
Smokescreen
   America, 5 May 1973, 420.
   Critic (May 1973): 82.
   Newsweek, 5 February 1973, 84.
   Observer, 15 October 1972, 38.
   Time, 5 March 1973, 75-Ell.
   Times Literary Supplement, 1 December 1972, 1467.
The Sport of Queens. See also entries under *Forfeit.*
   Christian Science Monitor, 17 July 1969, 5.
   Kirkus Reviews, 1 January 1969, 39.
   New York Times Book Review, 16 March 1969, 62.

Saturday Review, 16 August 1969, 59.
Trial Run
    Atlantic (July 1979): 82.
    New York Times, 20 May 1979, sec. VII, 34.
    New Yorker, 18 June 1979, 112.
    Observer, 22 October 1978, 35; 13 July 1980, 29.
    Progressive (August 1979): 60.
    Virginia Quarterly Review 55 (Autumn 1979): 138.
Twice Shy
    Book World, 18 April 1982, 6.
    Christian Science Monitor, 28 July 1982, 17.
    New York Times, 25 April 1982, sec. VII, 13.
    New Yorker, 17 May 1982, 141.
    Times Literary Supplement, 1 January 1982, 12.
Two by Francis [*Forfeit* and *Slayride*].
    New York Times, 8 February 1983, sec. III, 12.
Whip Hand
    New Republic, 28 June 1980, 40.
    New York, 21 April 1980, 83.
    New York Times, 8 June 1980, sec. VII, p. 31.
    New Yorker, 19 May 1980, 164.
    Progressive (October 1980): 59.
    Times Literary Supplement, 7 March 1980, 258.

Index